The Chesapeake Bay is the single most productive estuary in the United States, perhaps even the World. Since earliest times, the Bay has been fished, crabbed, tonged, dredged, sailed, dug in, swum in and hunted on. It is home to more than 2,000 species of animals and plants and serves as the basis of livelihood for hundreds of thousands of Maryland citizens.

The seafood industry is America's oldest, and as the third successful colony in English America, Marylanders have been catching, cooking and eating the Bay's delights for three and a half centuries. Of present day Maryland's twenty-three counties, only seven do not touch upon tidal waters.

But simply touching upon tidewater does not make Maryland unique. To understand the true relationship of Maryland and her waters one must fly over the State to see how the broad sloughs, coves, deep and sluggish rivers, wetlands and tidal ponds intermingle, embrace necks of lush, green land so that it becomes difficult to know if the land dominates the waters or the waters rule the land.

In Maryland, one finds an almost endless bounty from both land and water. Grains, fruits and vegetables thrive in the rich soil. Game abounds. And the grand Chesapeake—some 5,600 miles of tidal shoreline within the State—coupled with Maryland's Atlantic fisheries, produces an unprecedented richness in seafood.

Oysters. Clams. Crabs. Lobsters. Finfish of salt, brackish and fresh waters. Among lovers of seafood, Maryland has come to be as much adjective as noun, as much a style as a place. *Maryland* Crabcakes. *Maryland* Oyster Stew. *Maryland* Crab Soup. Maryland's seafood tradition is built upon more than a few ways to prepare a few species.

On the following pages, you will find many familiar shellfish and finfish species. You will also encounter new and different *fruits de mer* to excite your palate such as shark, eel and squid. Microwave methods of cookery, substitution of lower calorie ingredients and variety make this edition of Maryland Seafood Cookbooks a natural step after Cookbooks I and II.

Often overlooked, occasionally misunderstood, these new delicacies invite you to try them, for they too are part of Maryland's grand seafood tradition.

Gordon P. Hallock, Director, Office of Seafood Marketing

CRABS

The Blue Crab is one of the most flavorful crustaceans in the United States. Found along the Atlantic and Gulf Coasts living in bays, sounds and channels, they normally live in salt water but can be found in fresh or brackish water. The Chesapeake Bay is the largest producer of Blue Crabs in the world.

Blue Crabs migrate up the Bay during the spring and early summer. In the latter part of the summer these same crabs mate. The females migrate back down the Bay to spawn. After mating, the female may produce up to two million eggs. Only two or three of these eggs will survive and grow to maturity.

Growth of the Blue Crab is accomplished by molting. The crab sheds its hard shell under which is a new, soft shell. This is the delectable "soft shell crab."

After shedding, the soft shell will harden in about two hours, but only if left in the water. Crab season extends from April 1 to January 1. Maryland crabs are not harvested from January 1 to April 1 but crabmeat is still available through Maryland processors from other Blue Crab states.

Blue Crabs are marketed as both hard shells and soft shells. Soft shell crabs are considered a delicacy. The entire body of the soft shell may be eaten after dressing and cooking.

Hard shell crabs are sold live in the shell or they are steamed and the meat is picked and sold as canned or pasteurized crabmeat.

Picked crabmeat is marketed in several forms:

Lumpmeat or Backfin–Large whole lumps from the body.

Special–All meat from the body portion in normal proportions (includes lump and flake).

Flake (Regular)–All meat from the body portion except lump.

Claw–All meat from the claw appendages.

Crab Claws–Claws of the crab with the shell partially removed.

Pasteurized Crabmeat–Available in Backfin or Special.

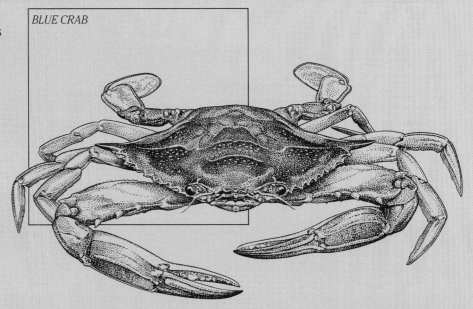

BLUE CRAB

Fresh crabmeat should be a white or lightly off-white color when purchased. It should have a fresh odor, a light "ocean" aroma. Once it starts to deteriorate, it takes on a "sour" smell, then ammonia. It also becomes darker in color with age. *Once the ammonia odor is detected the crabmeat should be discarded.*

Crabmeat is also marketed in pasteurized form. Pasteurization is a special heating process that prevents bacterial spoilage. The texture and flavor are not altered. Pasteurized crabmeat must be refrigerated. It can be stored for up to 6 months unopened in the refrigerator, but once it is opened it has a shelf life of only three to five days.

Fresh crabs bought in the shell must be alive before cooking. Live crabs stored in the refrigerator will become very sluggish due to the low temperature. However, once they are returned to room temperature, they will become more active.

Blue Crab has a mild, sweet tender taste and recipes using crab should consider its light flavor. It is very easily masked by overseasoning.

Species easily substituted for the Blue Crab include the Red Crab, King Crab and Tanner Crab.

The Blue Crab is the most important commercial species in Maryland but there are other crabs available on the market such as:

Stone Crab–found from North Carolina to the Gulf of Mexico. Most of the meat comes from the claws and the flavor is comparable to that of the Blue Crab.

Rock Crab–found along the North Atlantic coast from Nova Scotia to the south Atlantic states. The meat is equal to that of the Blue Crab in flavor and quantity.

Jonah Crab–found in the same areas as the Rock Crab. It has excellent flavor but distribution is limited.

Dungeness Crab–found along the Pacific Coast from Alaska to southern California. One of the largest edible crabs in the United States averaging nine inches in breadth.

Red Crab–found along the East Coast from Nova Scotia to Cuba. It has twice the yield of Blue Crab, as much as twenty-three percent more meat.

Alaska King Crab–found on both sides of the North Pacific Ocean, and on the western coast of North America.

Alaska Tanner Crab–found along the Eastern Pacific and Western Atlantic. It rivals the King Crab in size and flavor.

Live Blue Crabs purchased by the bushel are primarily male crabs, known locally as "jimmys." The female crabs, or "sooks," are usually sent to the crab houses and sold as picked meat. Live Blue Crabs are sold as: Jumbos, #1 Jimmys and Medium crabs. They also may be purchased as medium and large crabs. To be harvested, they must have a legal minimum shell size of five inches from point to point.

Soft shell crabs are a delicacy in Maryland and must be caught right after the crab has molted. They may be purchased live or frozen. See "freezing soft shell crabs" in the "Freezing Seafood" section of this book.

SPICY CRAB SOUP

1 quart water
3 chicken parts (neck or wing)
3 pounds canned tomatoes, quartered
8 ounces frozen corn, thawed
1 cup frozen peas, thawed
1 cup potatoes, diced
¾ cup celery, chopped
¾ cup onion, diced
¾ tablespoon seafood seasoning
1 teaspoon salt
¼ teaspoon lemon pepper
1 pound Maryland crabmeat, fresh or
  pasteurized, cartilage removed
  (regular or claw)

Place water and chicken in a 6 quart soup pot. Cover and simmer over low heat for at least one hour. Add vegetables and seasonings and simmer, covered, over medium low heat for about 45 minutes or until vegetables are almost done. Add crabmeat, cover and simmer for 15 more minutes or until hot. (If a milder soup is desired, decrease amount of seafood seasoning to 1-1½ teaspoons).

Yield: 8 servings. Calories: 153 per serving.

SOFT CRABS MIA

8 soft crabs, dressed
¼ cup soy sauce
1 ½ cups white wine
⅓ cup olive oil
2 tablespoons hot oil* (or 5-6 drops hot
  sauce)
2 garlic cloves, minced

* Hot oil may be purchased in gourmet
  sections in some major food stores

Mix together all ingredients except crabs in a shallow baking dish. Add crabs and cover. Marinate for ½ hour. Place crabs on a hot grill. Cook for 15 minutes on each side, basting and turning often. To decrease cooking time, cover grill with a large lid to help circulate the heat evenly. Crabs are cooked when red, firm and slightly crisp, but still moist.

Yield: 4 servings. Calories: 448 per serving.

CRAB CASSEROLE

2 tablespoons margarine
2 tablespoons flour
1 cup skim milk
10 drops hot sauce
2 tablespoons green pepper, diced
⅛ teaspoon lemon pepper seasoning
¼ teaspoon seafood seasoning
½ tablespoon worcestershire sauce
2 tablespoons parmesan cheese
2 tablespoons seasoned bread crumbs
2 tablespoons margarine
1 pound Maryland backfin crabmeat,
  cartilage removed

Microwave *(See page 35 "Terms for Microwaving")*:
Place margarine in a shallow casserole dish and microwave for 2 minutes. Blend in flour, then add milk, hot sauce, green pepper, seasonings and worcestershire sauce. Mix well. Cover and microwave on high for 6 minutes, stir. Fold in crabmeat. In a small bowl, microwave parmesan cheese, bread crumbs and margarine on roast for 2 minutes. Mix well and sprinkle over crabmeat, cover and microwave 4 minutes on high. Sprinkle with paprika.

Yield: 4 servings. Calories: 271 per serving.

CRAB ROLLS

½ pound Maryland regular crabmeat
1 teaspoon lemon juice
2 teaspoons soy sauce
¼ teaspoon seafood seasoning
½ cup red cabbage, shredded
½ cup fresh bean sprouts, diced
3 tablespoons onion, diced
2 tablespoons radish, minced
8 sheets phyllo dough 12" x 7", frozen
3 tablespoons oil

optional: mustard sauce or sweet n sour
  sauce

Preheat oven to 375°F. In a small bowl, gently toss crabmeat with lemon juice, soy sauce and seafood seasoning. In another small bowl, combine vegetables and mix well. Fold each sheet of phyllo dough in half, lengthwise. Pat lightly with a damp paper towel. Place 1½ tablespoons of crabmeat at one end of dough. Top with 1 tablespoon vegetable mixture. Roll up and seal ends. Place rolls on an oiled baking sheet. Bake until golden brown on each side, 15-20 minutes.

Yield: 8 rolls. Calories: 116 per roll.

CRAB STUFFED CHICKEN BREAST

6 3-ounce chicken breasts, skinned,
  boned
3 tablespoons low calorie mayonnaise
¼ teaspoon salt
⅛ teaspoon white pepper
¼ teaspoon seafood seasoning
1 pound Maryland regular crabmeat,
  cartilage removed
3 slices (½ ounce each) swiss cheese,
  cut in half
3 slices (½ ounce each) boiled ham,
  cut in half
⅔ cup flour
1 egg, mixed with 1 cup water
½ cup bread crumbs, mixed with: ½
  teaspoon each pepper, paprika
1 tablespoon parsley
4 tablespoons oil
paprika

Preheat oven to 400°F. Pound out chicken breasts to flatten to about ¼ inch thick. In a small bowl, combine mayonnaise and seasonings. Blend well. Gently stir in crabmeat. Mount about ¼-⅓ cup of crabmeat mixture on one end of each chicken breast. Top each with ½ slice of cheese and ½ slice of ham. Roll up and seal ends. Dip each in flour, then egg wash and bread crumb mixture. Heat 2 tablespoons oil in a large skillet and brown chicken breasts on both sides. Transfer to an oiled (2 tablespoons) baking sheet, sprinkle with paprika and bake for 10 minutes.

Yield: 6 servings. Calories: 274 each.

CRAB PATTIES

¼ cup plain, lowfat yogurt
2 tablespoons worcestershire sauce
1 teaspoon dry mustard
1 teaspoon salt
¼ teaspoon pepper
⅛ teaspoon seafood seasoning
1 large egg, beaten
1 pound Maryland regular crabmeat, fresh or pasteurized, cartilage removed
¼ cup stone wheat cracker crumbs
1½ tablespoons oil, for frying

In a small bowl, combine yogurt, worcestershire sauce, seasonings and egg. Pour mixture over crabmeat, add cracker crumbs and mix lightly. Mold mixture into 30 patties. Pan fry half of the patties in ¾ tablespoon oil, then add another ¾ tablespoon of oil for the remainder of the recipe. Patties are done when golden brown on each side. Serve with hot mustard sauce.

Yield: 30 crab patties. Calories: 28 calories each.

BRANDIED CRAB

1 pound Maryland backfin crabmeat, cartilage removed
2 tablespoons margarine
¼ cup fresh parsley, finely chopped
2 tablespoons brandy
⅛ teaspoon salt
⅛ teaspoon white pepper
pinch nutmeg
pinch paprika
1 large fresh lemon
1 loaf french bread, sliced thin

In a large skillet or electric wok, melt margarine. Add parsley, brandy, salt and white pepper, nutmeg, paprika and the juice of one lemon. Heat until hot. Add crabmeat and toss lightly to heat and coat. Be careful not to break up lumps. Arrange 2 slices of bread side by side on each serving plate. Mound crabmeat evenly on each slice of bread. May also be served with crackers as an hors d'oeuvre.

Yield: 4 servings. Calories: 264 per serving.

CRAB NEWBURG

¼ cup margarine
⅓ cup green pepper, diced
⅔ cup canned mushrooms, sliced
¼ cup flour
½ teaspoon salt
½ teaspoon dry mustard
pinch cayenne pepper
2 cups skim milk
¼ cup white wine
1 pound Maryland backfin crabmeat, cartilage removed
1 tablespoon grated parmesan cheese for sprinkling
fresh parsley, chopped, for sprinkling
paprika

Conventional oven:
Preheat oven to 350°. Melt margarine in a medium sauce pan. Add green pepper and mushrooms and saute for 5 minutes. In a small bowl, combine flour, salt, mustard and pepper. Blend into melted margarine. Add milk and wine and stir constantly until mixture thickens, 5-10 minutes. Mound crabmeat into 4 individual shells. Spoon about 3-4 tablespoons sauce over crabmeat. Sprinkle with paprika, grated parmesan cheese and parsley. Bake for about 7-9 minutes. Casserole dish may also be used.

Microwave (See page 35 "Terms for Microwaving"):
Place margarine, green pepper and mushrooms in a casserole dish. Microwave on roast for 3 minutes. In a small bowl, combine flour, salt, mustard and pepper. Blend into melted margarine. Add milk and wine and blend well. Cover and microwave for 7-9 minutes on roast stirring several times, until mixture thickens. Mound crabmeat in individual casseroles or shells. Pour 3-4 tablespoons sauce over each. Sprinkle with paprika, parsley and grated parmesan cheese. Microwave ½ of the shells at a time, on roast for 7-8 minutes, rotating shells positions every 3 minutes.

Yield: 4 servings. Calories: 307 per serving.

CRAB REGAL

½ pound Maryland backfin crabmeat, cartilage removed

Sauce:
¼ cup plain, lowfat yogurt
3 tablespoons catsup
½ tablespoon lemon juice
1 teaspoon worcestershire sauce
⅛ teaspoon salt
dash white pepper
⅛ teaspoon seafood seasoning

2 tablespoons fresh parsley, chopped
½ tablespoon seasoned bread crumbs

Conventional oven:
Pack crabmeat into 40 cleaned little neck clam shells. In a small bowl, mix together sauce ingredients. Spoon about ⅔ teaspoon of sauce over each hors d'oeuvre, covering all crabmeat. Sprinkle each with parsley and bread crumbs. Place under preheated broiler for 2-3 minutes, just until hot.

Microwave (See page 35 "Terms for Microwaving"):
Follow above directions except for cooking method. Place ½ (20) of recipe on plate. Microwave on high for 1 minute, 30 seconds. Serve immediately. Microwave remaining hors d'oeuvres.

Yield: 40 hors d'oeuvres. Calories: 8 calories each.

CRAB STUFFED MUSHROOMS

20 large mushroom caps, cleaned, stems removed
2 tablespoons plain, lowfat yogurt
1 large egg, beaten
2 teaspoons onion, diced
¼ teaspoon seafood seasoning
2 teaspoons parsley, finely chopped
1 teaspoon worcestershire sauce
1½ tablespoons lemon juice
⅛ teaspoon salt
½ pound Maryland backfin crabmeat, cartilage removed
parmesan cheese and paprika for sprinkling

Conventional oven:
Arrange the mushroom caps in a shallow casserole dish (line with 3 layers of paper towels if microwaving). In a medium bowl, mix together the remaining ingredients and gently fold in crabmeat. Stuff each mushroom cap, forming a mound of stuffing ½″ over the top of the mushroom. Sprinkle with parmesan cheese and paprika. To bake, preheat oven to 425° and bake for 8-10 minutes.

Microwave *(See page 35 "Terms for Microwaving")*:
Line a shallow casserole dish with 3 layers of paper towels. Place 10 mushrooms at a time in dish and microwave on roast for 3 minutes. Repeat with remaining mushrooms, serve on a garnished platter.

Yield: 20 mushrooms. Calories: 20 each.

STUFFED CHERRY TOMATOES

15 ripe cherry tomatoes, washed
¼ pound Maryland backfin crabmeat
2 teaspoons plain, lowfat yogurt
1 teaspoon parsley, chopped
1 teaspoon onion, finely diced
½ teaspoon worcestershire sauce
⅛ teaspoon seafood seasoning
pinch salt
⅛ teaspoon white pepper
parsley
paprika

Core tops of tomatoes, set aside. Combine remaining ingredients and mix gently. Spoon mixture into tomatoes, filling about ½ inch over tomato tops. Sprinkle lightly with paprika and parsley. Serve cold or hot. To heat, bake in a preheated 375° oven for 10 minutes.

Variations:
Filling can also be used to stuff celery or other raw vegetables or to serve on crackers.

Yield: 15 tomatoes. Calories: 15 each.

1 cup zucchini, quartered and sliced thin
⅓ cup green pepper, finely chopped
1 cup fresh mushrooms, sliced thin
1 teaspoon olive oil
1 pound Maryland backfin crabmeat,
    cartilage removed
6 large eggs
½ teaspoon salt
¼ teaspoon pepper
¼ teaspoon Italian seasoning
2 tablespoons fresh parsley, chopped
½ cup mild cheddar cheese, grated
paprika for sprinkling

In a large skillet, saute zucchini, green pepper, and mushrooms in oil until slightly soft. Distribute vegetables evenly over the skillet surface. Sprinkle crab evenly over vegetables. Heat thoroughly over medium low 2 minutes. In a medium bowl, beat eggs with electric mixer or wisk until blended. Stir in spices. Pour egg mixture evenly over crabmeat. Sprinkle with parsley, cheese and paprika. Cover with a lid and cook over low heat until bottom is lightly golden and cheese is melted.

Yield: 4 servings. Calories: 304 per serving.

½ cup plain, lowfat yogurt
6 ounces cream cheese, softened
2 tablespoons low calorie mayonnaise
1 tablespoon lemon juice
1 teaspoon worcestershire sauce
½ teaspoon beau monde
½ teaspoon dry mustard
2 tablespoons milk
¼ cup cheddar cheese, grated
½ pound Maryland regular crabmeat,
    cartilage removed
paprika for sprinkling

Conventional oven:
In a double broiler or electric fondue pot, combine all ingredients except the crabmeat. Stir over medium-low heat until cheeses melt. Gently fold in crabmeat and heat thoroughly. Sprinkle with paprika. Serve hot with raw vegetables, crackers or party breads.

Microwave *(See page 35 "Terms for Microwaving")*:
Combine all ingredients, except for crabmeat, in a glass bowl. Cover and microwave on roast for 6 minutes. Gently fold in crabmeat, cover and microwave for 3 minutes on roast. Sprinkle with paprika.

Yield: 2½ cups. Calories: 30 per tablespoon.

SPRING CRAB SALAD

2 pineapples, cut in half length-wise,
    center scooped out
1 pound Maryland backfin crabmeat,
    cartilage removed
1 cup pineapple, chopped
½ cup chickpeas (optional)
½ cup fresh parsley, chopped
¼ cup walnuts, chopped
2 medium apples, sliced ¼"
2 tablespoons lemon juice
lettuce or romaine

Celery Seed Dressing:
½ cup cider vinegar
¾ cup salad oil
3½ tablespoons confectioners sugar
½ teaspoon salt
½ teaspoon paprika
¼ cup onion, chopped
¼ cup pineapple
½ tablespoon celery seed

Prepare pineapples. In a medium bowl, combine crabmeat, pineapple, chickpeas, parsley and walnuts and toss gently. Slice apples and cover with lemon juice. Line pineapples with lettuce or romaine. Mound ¼ of the crab mixture on each lettuce bed. Arrange apple slices around crab mixture. Top with a small piece of apple. Refrigerate until ready to serve. To make dressing, combine all ingredients in a blender and liquify. Refrigerate and serve chilled.

Yield (Salad): 4 servings. Calories (Salad): 312 per serving.

Yield (Dressing): 1½ cups. Calories (Dressing): 67 per tablespoon.

ASPARAGUS AND CRAB SOUP

½ cup margarine
½ cup flour
8 cups skim milk
2 tablespoons onion, finely chopped
2 teaspoons instant chicken bouillon
½ teaspoon pepper
½ teaspoon nutmeg
½ teaspoon paprika
1 teaspoon salt
2 teaspoons parsley flakes
10 ounces frozen asparagus, thawed,
    cut in thirds
1 pound Maryland regular crabmeat,
    cartilage removed

Melt margarine in a large sauce pan over medium heat. Gradually blend in flour. Stir in milk and add onion, bouillon, seasonings and parsley. Continue stirring until mixture thickens slightly. Add asparagus and cook over medium-low heat for 20-30 minutes, stirring often. Add crabmeat and cook over medium heat for 5 minutes. Serve hot.

Yield: 6 servings. Calories: 379 per serving.

1 egg
¼ cup low calorie mayonnaise
¼ cup plain, lowfat yogurt
½ tablespoon worcestershire sauce
6-7 drops hot sauce
½ teaspoon salt
½ teaspoon seafood seasoning
1 pound Maryland backfin crabmeat,
  cartilage removed
½ tablespoon parmesan cheese
paprika for sprinkling
fresh lemon wedges

Preheat oven to 400°. In a medium bowl, mix together egg, mayonnaise, yogurt, sauces and seasonings. Gently fold crabmeat into mixture. Spoon into individual shells. Sprinkle with cheese then paprika. Bake for about 15 minutes until hot and bubbly. Garnish.

Yield: 4 servings. Calories: 165 per serving.

DIJON CRAB SALAD

½ pound Maryland backfin crabmeat,
    cartilage removed
1 tablespoon carrots, shredded
⅓ cup celery, diced
⅓ cup cucumber, sliced thin
¼ cup apple with skin, diced
romaine lettuce leaves

Dijon dressing:
1 cup salad oil
¼ cup Dijon mustard
¼ cup white wine tarragon vinegar
1 teaspoon persillade

Gently toss together crabmeat, vegetables and apple.* Serve salad on a bed of romaine lettuce. Mix together all the dressing ingredients. Stir until blended. Serve with dressing.

Yield: 4 servings. Calories: 66 per serving. 85 calories per 1 tablespoon dressing.

*To prevent apple from turning brown, dip it in a mixture of 1 tablespoon lemon juice and 1 cup water.

SHE CRAB SOUP

3 tablespoons margarine
3 tablespoons flour
6 cups skim milk
2 teaspoons soy sauce
2 teaspoons worcestershire sauce
¼ cup sherry
½ teaspoon white pepper
½ teaspoon salt
¼ teaspoon thyme
pinch seafood seasoning
1 whole bay leaf
10 ounces frozen mixed vegetables,
    thawed and drained
1 pound Maryland regular crabmeat,
    cartilage removed

Melt margarine in a large sauce pan over low heat. Add flour gradually and blend well. Add milk 1 cup at a time, stirring continuously until well blended. Add sauces, sherry and seasonings. Simmer, covered, for 35-45 minutes. Add vegetables. Cook over medium heat for 10 minutes. Stir in the crabmeat and cook over medium heat until hot.

Yield: 4 servings. Calories: 410 per serving.

CRAB TARTS

pastry for 2 crust pie
3 large eggs, beaten
1½ cups skim milk
¾ cup swiss cheese, grated
2 tablespoons cream cheese, softened
1 tablespoon onion, minced
¼ cup fresh parsley, chopped fine
½ cup carrots, shredded
1 pound Maryland regular crabmeat,
    cartilage removed
½ teaspoon nutmeg
¼ teaspoon white pepper
pinch salt

Roll out dough thinly and cut out 2″ diameter circles with a cookie cutter. Lightly press dough circles into oiled tart shells. Prick dough with a fork. Bake for 5-7 minutes at 450°F. Remove from oven. Set aside. Mix together remaining ingredients and spoon into tart shells, filling them ½″ over the top of the tart shell. Bake for 25 minutes at 375°F. or until a toothpick inserted comes out clean. Serve hot.

Yield: 60 tarts. Calories: 52 each.

CRAB SOUFFLE

¼ cup margarine
¼ cup flour
1 tablespoon onion, finely chopped
⅛ teaspoon salt
¼ teaspoon tarragon leaves, crushed
⅛ teaspoon seafood seasoning
1 ½ teaspoons parsley flakes
⅓ cup medium cheddar cheese, grated
1 cup skim milk
½ pound Maryland regular crabmeat,
    cartilage removed
3 eggs, separated
¼ teaspoon cream of tartar
paprika to garnish

Preheat oven to 325°. Butter a 2-quart souffle dish. Melt butter in a large sauce pan over low heat. Gradually stir in flour until well blended. Cook over medium heat until mixture is bubbly. Add onion and spices. Stir in cheese and milk and cook until cheese has melted. Remove from heat. Add crabmeat to mixture. Beat egg yolks until thick and pour into the crab mixture, stir gently. Beat egg whites with cream of tartar until stiff. Gently fold egg whites into the crab mixture. Spoon mixture into a lightly greased souffle dish. Bake in oven about 35-40 minutes or until knife inserted in the center comes out clean.

Yield: 4 servings. Calories: 308 per serving.

CRAB CAKES (MICROWAVED/BROILED)

½ cup cracker crumbs
1 large egg, beaten
¼ cup plus 2 tablespoons low calorie
    mayonnaise
1 teaspoon worcestershire sauce
1 ½ teaspoons prepared mustard
½ teaspoon seafood seasoning
¼ teaspoon pepper
1 tablespoon onion, minced
1 tablespoon celery, finely chopped
2 tablespoons parsley, finely chopped
1 pound Maryland regular crabmeat,
    cartilage removed
1 tablespoon oil
paprika for garnish

Conventional oven:
Mix together all ingredients except crabmeat in a medium size bowl. Fold crabmeat in gently. Shape into 8 crab cakes. To broil, preheat broiler. Sprinkle crab cakes with paprika and place on a lightly oiled (with 1 tablespoon) baking sheet. Broil 4-6 inches away from heat source until golden brown.

Microwave *(See page 35 "Terms for Microwaving")*:
Only use ½ tablespoon oil to brush on large flat plate. Microwave plate for 2 minutes on high to heat oil. Place cakes on plate, sprinkle with paprika and microwave for 7 minutes on high.

Yield: 4 servings, 2 crab cakes each. Calories: 351 per serving.

OYSTERS

The term "oysters" refers to more than a hundred species of bivalved mollusks. True oysters have dissimilar lower and upper shells or valves, which are hinged together. Oysters were one of the earliest seafoods used by man.

The following are some of the most important species of oysters:

Eastern, Atlantic or American Oyster: Commercially the Eastern Oyster is the most important species, accounting for approximately 85% of the total production in the U.S. They are found along the North Atlantic seaboard to the Gulf of Mexico.

Pacific; or Pacific King Oyster: Grows in coastal waters from Alaska to Northern California, with the biggest production areas in the state of Washington.

Western or Olympia Oyster: The Western oyster is native to the Pacific Coast. The yield of this species has declined because of overharvesting and predation.

Oysters are available in several forms: live in the shell, fresh shucked, frozen and canned. Shucked oysters may be purchased in gallon, quart, pint and half-pints. Live oysters may be purchased by the bushel, 1/2 bushel, peck, 1/2 peck and by the dozen.

Oysters in the shell must be alive when purchased. This is indicated by a tightly closed shell. If the shell remains gapped after tapping, discard it.

Oysters can be eaten year around because of present day refrigeration. Formerly, oysters were only eaten during months having an "r" in their name. This old "R Rule" is no longer followed, and availability alone now governs when and how oysters may be eaten.

Oysters are still harvested from private beds after the season has ended. Modern shipping and refrigeration have enabled the oyster to be frozen and kept under proper temperatures to insure wholesomeness to the consumer. More and more, oysters are being served in restaurants year round because of the modern day refrigeration.

Oysters are very low in calories, only 19 calories per ounce, and contain protein, calcium, phosphorous, iron, potassium, Vitamin A, and thiamin. They are savored raw on the half shell, baked, broiled, steamed, stewed, fried or used in stuffings.

Oysters have a mild flavor; do not overpower this delicacy with seasonings. The oyster's flavor is best brought out when served in a cream sauce.

Remember that the tender meat of the oyster cooks in just seconds. They should be cooked only long enough to heat throughout, using a low to medium temperature, and they are done when the edges begin to curl.

Oysters turn many different colors for a variety of reasons: what the oyster has eaten or a rapid change in temperature. The most commonly found colors of fresh shucked oysters may be described as creamy, gray, brownish, pale yellow, red, green, or a combination of these colors. They are quite safe to eat.

When you store fresh oysters in the shell in the refrigerator, leave the grit and dirt on them. This helps insulate and keep the oysters moist. When ready to shuck, run under cold water, and scrub with a stiff brush.

TWO EASY WAYS OF OPENING AN OYSTER

"Billing" Method

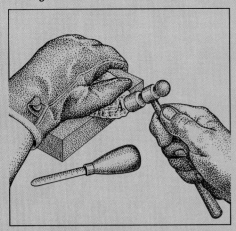

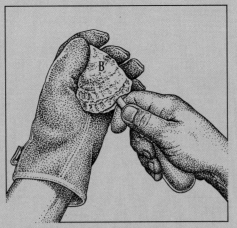

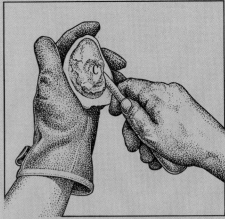

1. Hold oyster deep shell down, place edge of shell on block with shell extending over block, break shell at "A."

2. Insert blade between shells and cut muscle at "B." Pry upper shell off, using blade as lever.

3. Hold under faucet and wash out all grit and shell fragments.

4. Cut muscle from lower shell at "C" and oyster is now ready to serve.

"Side-Knife" Method

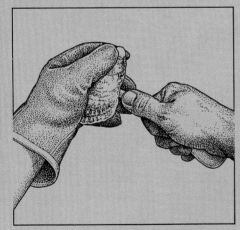

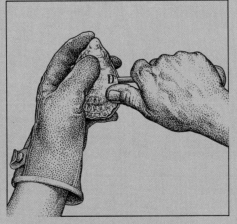

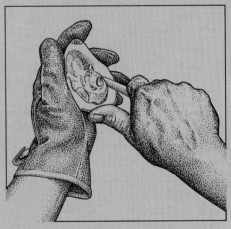

1. Hold oyster deep shell down. Hold knife with thumb extended to within 1/4″ of the point.

2. Place point of knife a trifle inside the outer edge of upper shell. Wriggle knife down and in between shells.

3. Push blade across under upper shell and cut muscle at "D." Keep thumb on oyster and pry shell off.

4. Hold under faucet and wash out all grit and shell fragments.

5. Cut muscle from lower shell at "C" and oyster is now ready to serve.

How to Open Oysters in a Microwave*

Scrub oysters under running water. Place oysters in a glass casserole dish. Microwave on warm for 5 minutes. Remove from oven and shuck immediately. Oysters are uncooked.

To completely open an oyster, microwave for 3 minutes on high. Meat will be thoroughly cooked.

*See page 35 "Terms for Microwaving"

CLAMS

Like oysters, clams are bivalve mollusks. They are found in fresh and salt waters. There are about 20,000 kinds of clams but only about 50 varieties are large, tasty and abundant enough to be commercially harvested.

Some of the most important species of clams are:

Surf Clam–The surf clam is harvested in greater numbers than other species. Though abundant along Atlantic shores, it is not as valuable as the hard or soft shell clam. Most canned clams are surf clams.

Ocean Quahog–It is commonly referred to as the "Mahogany Clam," "Mahogany Quahog," and "Black Quahog." The ocean quahog has a hard shell that is extremely difficult to open with a knife.

Hard Clam–is found along the Atlantic and Gulf coasts to Texas.

Soft Shell Clam–The soft shell clam is known in the Chesapeake Bay area as a "Manninose," "Long Clam" and "Long Neck." The shell is elongated, thin and brittle.

Geoduck Clam–A Pacific Coast clam, the geoduck has been recently utilized as a commercial resource.

Clams are harvested year round with soft clams being most abundant in the spring. Clams are available alive in the shell, fresh shucked, frozen or canned. Shucked clams are generally sold by the pint or quart.

Clam juice, broth and nectar are also available canned or bottled. Fresh and canned clams can be used interchangeably in recipes.

Clams should be alive when purchased, this is evident when the shells are tightly closed. Shucked clams should be plump, with clear liquor and free from shell particles.

The hard clam is marketed in several sizes. From smallest to largest: Littlenecks, Cherrystones and Chowders. Generally, the larger the clam the tougher the meat.

If you gather clams from the shore yourself, you must first wash off all surface sand with water and brush away debris with a hard brush. Cover clams with a solution of 1/3 cup salt in 1 gallon of tap water. The sand will settle to the bottom. Change the water and repeat this process two or three times. Do not allow clams to remain in water for longer than 30 minutes at a time.

FOUR WAYS TO SHUCK A HARD CLAM:

1. Wash clams. Hold the clam in the palm of one hand with the hinge against palm. Insert a slender knife between the halves of the shell (much as you would open an oyster) and cut around the clam, twisting the knife to pry open the shell. Cut both muscles from the shell.

2. Wash clams as above and place them in a small amount of boiling water. Cover and steam for 5-10 minutes or until they are partially opened. Remove, cool and shuck quickly.

3. Put the clams in the freezer for 5-10 minutes. Remove and shuck immediately. Cold relaxes the muscle of the clam and should make it easier to shuck.

4. Place about 10 clams in the microwave oven. Microwave* on warm for 12 minutes. Remove clams that have partially opened. Continue microwaving remaining clams on warm at 1 minute intervals until they all open partially. Shuck immediately.

*See page 35 "Terms for Microwaving"

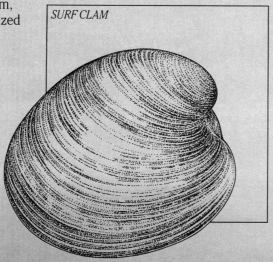

SURF CLAM

Photo opposite: Oysters Vanderbeek

2 tablespoons olive oil
2 tablespoons margarine
2 green onions, chopped
1 clove garlic, minced
1 tablespoon parsley, chopped
½ cup water chestnuts, sliced thin
pinch white pepper
pinch crushed red pepper
¼ teaspoon salt
¼ cup white wine
½ tablespoon flour
½ cup oyster liquor
1 pint shucked Maryland standard
    oysters, drained
4 cups cooked linguine noodles

Heat oil and margarine in a large skillet on medium low setting. Add onions, garlic, parsley and saute until slightly soft. Add water chestnuts, spices and wine and cook for 3-4 minutes. Blend in flour and oyster liquor and mix well. Add oysters and allow to simmer for 5 minutes stirring twice. (More red pepper may be added for extra seasoning). Serve over linguine.

Yield: 4 servings. Calories: 428 per serving (includes linguine).

2 pints Maryland standard oysters
1 cup white vinegar
¼ cup sugar
2 teaspoons tarragon
3 tablespoons pickling spice
¼ cup sherry
crackers

Conventional oven:
In a large sauce pan, simmer oysters in liquor until curled. Set aside. Combine remaining ingredients in a small sauce pan and cook over medium heat for 10 minutes. Drain oysters thoroughly and transfer to a bowl. Strain sauce and pour liquid over oysters. Cover and refrigerate for at least 3 hours. Serve with crackers.

Microwave *(See page 35 "Terms for Microwaving")*:
Place oysters and liquor in a shallow baking dish. Cover and microwave on roast for 5 minutes or until oysters curl. Combine marinade ingredients in a separate bowl, cover and microwave for 4 minutes on high. Strain and pour into a bowl. Drain oysters and add to marinade. Refrigerate three hours.

Yield: 40 oysters. Calories: 22 each.

OYSTERS ARUNDEL

1 pint Maryland standard oysters,
   drained and cut into thirds
1 green onion, chopped
6 slices bacon, ¾ cooked and
   crumbled
dash onion powder for each
dash lemon pepper for each
2 teaspoons bread crumbs
dash worcestershire sauce for each
2 ounces cheddar cheese,
   finely grated

Conventional oven:
Preheat oven to 350°F. Place 16 individual shells on a large baking pan. Place 2-3 pieces of oyster on each shell. Sprinkle each with green onion, bacon, spices, bread crumbs, and worcestershire sauce. Top with a sprinkling of cheddar cheese. Bake for about 10 minutes or until cheese is melted. Serve hot.

Microwave *(See page 35 "Terms for Microwaving")*:
Place oyster pieces on 16 individual shells. Sprinkle each with onion, bacon, spices, bread crumbs, and worcestershire sauce. Top each with a sprinkling of cheddar cheese. Cook half (8) at a time in microwave. Microwave on roast for about 3-4 minutes.

This can also be made on party size bread slices instead of in individual shells.

Yield: 16 oysters. Calories: 45 calories per oyster.

STATEHOUSE OYSTER CHOWDER

4 strips bacon
2 cups water
1 cup potatoes, diced
1 cup carrots, chopped
½ cup onions, diced
1½ cups frozen corn, thawed
1½ cups frozen peas, thawed
1 cup celery, chopped
2 cups skim milk
½ cup fresh parsley, finely chopped
1 teaspoon oregano
1½ teaspoons salt
¼ teaspoon pepper
2 tablespoons worcestershire sauce
¼ cup cornstarch
1 quart Maryland standard oysters, cut
   into thirds

Cook bacon in a large sauce pan over medium heat until half-cooked. Transfer to paper towels, crumble when cool. Wipe out sauce pan and pour in water. Add all vegetables, bacon, cover and simmer until almost done. Add 1 cup milk, parsley, spices and worcestershire sauce. Pour remaining cup of milk into a small bowl, gradually blend in cornstarch and mix well. Pour cornstarch mixture into the large sauce pan and stir until well blended. Add oysters, cover and simmer for 15 more minutes or until oysters curl.

Yield: 6 servings. Calories: 217 per serving.

OYSTERS ANNAPOLIS

18 Maryland oysters in shell*
1 egg yolk
½ cup green pepper, chopped
2 tablespoons pimento, chopped
1 teaspoon dry mustard
¼ cup mayonnaise
1 tablespoon worcestershire sauce
½ teaspoon salt
¼ teaspoon white pepper
1 pound Maryland regular crabmeat,
    fresh or pasteurized, cartilage
    removed

*fresh shucked oysters can also be used

Open oysters and separate from shell. Cut each one into 4 small pieces and place in the deeper shell. In a medium mixing bowl, combine remaining ingredients, except for crabmeat and mix well. Add crabmeat and stir gently and thoroughly.

Conventional oven:
To bake, top each oyster with about 3 tablespoons of crab meat mixture. Place shells on a baking pan and bake in oven for 20 minutes on 350°F.

Microwave (See page 35 "Terms for Microwaving"):
Microwave shucked oysters in ½ shell for 2-3 minutes on roast (only half at a time). Top each oyster with crabmeat mixture, sprinkle with paprika and microwave for 3-5 minutes on roast, rotating shells once. Drain off excess moisture and serve hot. Repeat for remaining oysters.

Yield: Makes approximately 18 oysters. Calories: 68 per oyster.

OYSTERS ROCKEFELLER

20 oysters, in shell
8 strips bacon
4 tablespoons margarine
4 tablespoons celery, chopped fine
4 tablespoons onion, chopped fine
2 tablespoons parsley, chopped
5 ounces spinach, chopped, thawed, and
    well drained
1 tablespoon anisette
½ tablespoon margarine
2 tablespoons bread crumbs
rock salt

Preheat oven to 450°F. Shuck oysters. Leave oysters in deep half of shell. Fry bacon until slightly crisp, drain on paper towels. Chop bacon finely and set aside. In margarine, saute celery, onion and parsley until slightly tender. Remove sauteed vegetables from stove, add spinach and anisette. Line baking trays with rock salt, ¼" deep. Place oysters in shells in rock salt and pack down. Sprinkle 1 teaspoon spinach mixture over each oyster. Sprinkle ½ teaspoon finely chopped bacon over each. Melt ½ tablespoon butter and mix in bread crumbs. Sprinkle lightly on oysters. Bake for 10 minutes. Serve.

Yield: 20 oysters. Calories: 48 for each oyster.

OYSTERS ROMANO

½ cup margarine, melted
1½ teaspoons bread crumbs
1 teaspoon lemon juice
2 tablespoons green onion, chopped
3 tablespoons almond slivers, chopped
2 teaspoons anisette
1 teaspoon pimento, chopped
pinch salt and white pepper
½ teaspoon seafood seasoning
4 teaspoons parsley, finely chopped
1 pint or 16 oysters, raw
romano cheese, grated
parsley for garnish
1 pimento, chopped

Conventional oven:
In a small bowl, blend together margarine and bread crumbs. Mix in lemon juice, green onion, almonds, anisette, pimento, spices and chopped parsley. Place 16 raw oysters on 16 scalloped shells or on the half shell. Spoon about 1 tablespoon mixture over each oyster. Sprinkle each oyster with 1 teaspoon romano cheese. Garnish with parsley and chopped pimento. Place oysters on a baking sheet and bake for 10 minutes at 425°F. Serve.

Microwave (See page 35 "Terms for Microwaving"):
Instead of baking oysters, microwave 8 oysters at a time 4½ to 5 minutes on simmer. Rotate oysters after 2 minutes. Repeat. Serve.

Yield: 16 oysters. Calories: 82 per oyster.

Crepe batter:
¾ cup flour
pinch white pepper
2 eggs, beaten
⅔ cup skim milk
1 tablespoon oil

Crepe filling:
¼ cup margarine
¼ cup flour
½ cup skim milk
3 ounces cream cheese, softened
1 tablespoon green onion, chopped
2 teaspoons green pepper
1 tablespoon pimento
¼ teaspoon celery salt
¼ teaspoon sage
¼ teaspoon white pepper
1 pint Maryland standard oysters,
　shucked

Crepe sauce:
2 tablespoons pimento, chopped
⅔ cup plus 2 tablespoons skim milk

Crepe batter:
Mix flour and pepper in a small bowl, make a hollow in the center. Mix together eggs, milk and oil and gradually add this to the flour, stirring constantly. Spoon out 1 tablespoon of batter onto a small oiled skillet and cook at medium high until lightly golden (cook one side only). Layer between paper towels in a warm oven until ready to use.

Filling:
Melt margarine in a small sauce pan. Gradually stir in flour. Add milk and cream cheese. Cook over medium heat until smooth. Stir in onion, pepper, pimento and spices. Measure out ½ cup of filling and put this in another small sauce pan (to be used for sauce). Drain oysters well on paper towels. Chop oysters in half and add them to the remaining filling mixture. Heat mixture over medium-low heat until thoroughly hot.

Sauce:
Add milk and chopped pimento to the ½ cup filling mixture that was set aside. Cook over medium low heat until smooth and hot.

Fill crepe shells with oyster filling mixture. Roll up crepe placing seam side down. Pour hot sauce over top. Serve immediately.

Yield: 8 crepes, 2 per serving. Calories: 249 per crepe.

---

2 tablespoons olive oil
1 clove garlic, minced
2 tablespoons black olives, chopped
3 tablespoons green pepper, chopped
3 tablespoons onion, chopped
3 tablespoons celery, chopped
1 tablespoon plus 2 teaspoons flour
1 16-ounce can stewed tomatoes
¼ cup dry red wine
¼ cup dry white wine
½ cup oyster liquor
⅛ teaspoon white pepper
½ teaspoon celery salt
1 teaspoon Italian herbs
1 pint shucked Maryland standard
　oysters, cut in half
4 cups cooked long grain rice

Saute garlic, olives, green pepper, onion, and celery in oil until slightly soft. Add flour, stirring quickly to avoid lumping. Add tomatoes, wines and oyster liquor. Stir over low heat until blended. Add spices. Add oysters and cook over medium heat for about 10 minutes, stirring often. Serve over rice.

Yield: 4 servings. Calories: 384 per serving (includes rice).

CURRIED OYSTER CHOWDER

1 cube chicken bouillon
½ cup water, boiling
1 cup potatoes, shredded
1 medium onion, diced
½ cup carrots, shredded
½ cup celery, diced
1 tablespoon margarine, melted
1 tablespoon flour
1 cup skim milk
1 teaspoon salt
1 pint Maryland standard oysters, cut in half
1 teaspoon curry powder
4 ounces Monterey Jack cheese, cut in cubes

Dissolve bouillon cube in boiling water. Pour into a large sauce pan. Add vegetables and simmer until slightly soft. In a small bowl, blend melted margarine and flour. Add to vegetables. Pour in skim milk and simmer for 5 minutes. Add salt and oysters and simmer for 10 more minutes. Stir in curry powder. Place cheese cubes in the bottom of 4 soup bowls. Pour hot chowder over cheese cubes.

Yield: Serves 4-12 ounce portions. Calories: 270 per serving.

BEER BATTER FRIED OYSTERS

2 cups bisquick mix
2 teaspoons parsley
¼ teaspoon seafood seasoning
1 cup beer
2 large eggs, beaten
¼ cup oil
2 pints shucked Maryland standard oysters,* drained
½ cup oyster liquor
¼ cup oil for frying

*soft shell clams may also be fried in this batter

Mix bisquick and seasonings in a small bowl. Add beer, eggs and oil and mix well. Cover with plastic and allow mixture to stand at room temperature for 1 hour. Add ½ cup oyster liquor to beer batter mixture. Heat oil in an electric skillet at 275°F-300°F. Dip oysters in batter and drop onto hot skillet. Fry several at a time until golden brown on both sides. Drain and serve.

Yield: 6 servings. Calories: 424 per serving.

OYSTER GRAVY AND BISCUITS

1 pint Maryland standard oysters
2 tablespoons margarine
2 tablespoons flour
1 cup oyster liquor, add water if necessary
3 tablespoons white wine
1 clove garlic, minced
1 tablespoon worcestershire sauce
1 tablespoon green pepper, diced
¼ teaspoon salt
⅛ teaspoon pepper
1 teaspoon bacon bits

1 dozen hot biscuits

In a sauce pan, simmer oysters in liquor until curled. Drain, reserving 1 cup of liquor and set aside. In a medium sauce pan, melt margarine and blend flour gradually. Add reserved liquor and remaining ingredients except oysters. Stir over medium heat until thickened. Add oysters and heat thoroughly. Spoon gravy over hot biscuits.

Yield: 4 servings. Calories: 472 per serving, includes 3 biscuits.

24 Maryland Littleneck clams in shell
6 slices bacon
¼ cup onion, minced
⅓ cup green pepper, minced
3 tablespoons chives, chopped
3 tablespoons grated parmesan cheese
1 tablespoon lemon juice
¼ teaspoon white pepper
⅛ teaspoon seafood seasoning
1 teaspoon paprika

rock salt
lemon slices and parsley for garnish

Conventional oven:
Preheat oven to 400°F. Shuck clams, reserving liquid. Remove clam and cut into 3 pieces. Place back on one side of shell. Saute bacon until slightly crisp. Drain and crumble. In a small bowl, mix together bacon and remaining ingredients. Place about 1 teaspoon of mixture on each clam. Spread a layer of rock salt ½ inch deep on a baking sheet. Mold clams into rock salt and bake for about 10 minutes. Garnish and serve hot.

Microwave *(See page 35 "Terms for Microwaving")*:
Open clams (8 at a time) by microwaving on warm for 3 minutes. Place rock salt on a microwave dish and arrange 8 prepared clams on rock salt. Microwave 8 at a time on roast for 3 minutes. Garnish and serve hot.

Yield: 24 clams. Calories: 24 per clam.

CLAMS MORNAY

6 patty shells, frozen
¾ cup soft shell clams, drained, chopped
¾ cup fresh mushrooms, sliced
2 tablespoons white wine
1 tablespoon margarine
1 tablespoon flour
¼ cup plus 2 tablespoons clam juice
½ teaspoon lemon juice
½ cup Gruyere cheese, grated
1½ tablespoons carrot, shredded
1½ tablespoons watercress or parsley, chopped
pinch white pepper
¼ teaspoon salt
dash cayenne pepper

Bake patty shells according to package directions. Remove center pieces. Heat oven to 375°. Saute clams and mushrooms in wine for 3-4 minutes. Drain and spoon into patty shells. In a small sauce pan, melt margarine and blend in flour. Stir over medium heat until bubbly. Stir in clam and lemon juices and heat for 4-5 minutes. Add cheese, carrots, watercress and spices and mix well. Heat for 2-3 minutes or until cheese is melted. Spoon hot sauce over clams and mushrooms. Bake in oven for 10 minutes. Serve immediately.

Yield: 3 servings/2 shells each. Calories: 482 per serving.

MANHATTAN STYLE CLAM CHOWDER

1 cup potatoes, peeled and chopped
1⅔ cups water
2 1-pound cans tomatoes, chopped
1 cup celery, chopped
⅔ cup green pepper, chopped
1 10-ounce package frozen cut green beans, thawed
1 tablespoon margarine
1½ cups clam juice
¼ cup bacon bits
2 tablespoons catsup
1 tablespoon worcestershire sauce
1½ teaspoons Italian herbs
¼ teaspoon thyme
½ teaspoon basil
salt and pepper to taste
2 bay leaves
1 cup or 16 Cherrystone clams, shucked, drained and finely chopped

In a large sauce pan, boil potatoes in water for 10 minutes. Add remaining ingredients except clams. Allow to simmer on medium-low heat for 45 minutes. Add clams and simmer for 5 more minutes. Serve.

Yield: 5 servings. Calories: 229 per serving.

ZESTY CLAM HORS D'OEUVRES

14 Cherrystone clams, shucked
    and chopped
1 tablespoon onion, minced
1 ½ tablespoons green pepper, minced
Dash oregano, garlic powder, pepper
1 tablespoon parmesan cheese
1 tablespoon Italian bread crumbs
hot sauce (drop for each)
2 tablespoons almonds, crumbled
2 teaspoons pimento, chopped

Conventional oven:
In a small bowl mix all ingredients except clams. Preheat oven to 450°F. Place chopped clams on half shells. Sprinkle clams evenly with mixture, bake in oven for 10-12 minutes.

Microwave *(See page 35 "Terms for Microwaving")*:
Prepare as above. Place 7 shells on a plate, cover with plastic and microwave for 3-4 minutes on roast.

Yield: 14 clams. Calories: 25 each.

CLAM CAKES

1 teaspoon olive oil
2 tablespoons onion, minced
¼ cup celery, minced
½ cup cracker crumbs
1 large egg, beaten
pinch pepper
¼ teaspoon dry mustard
⅛ teaspoon each seafood seasoning,
    garlic powder (use ¼ teaspoon
    for spicier cakes)
¼ teaspoon salt
¼ cup chopped parsley
1 cup clams, chopped and drained
    (hard or soft clams may be used)

Conventional oven:
Preheat oven to 425°F. Saute vegetables in oil for about 3-5 minutes. In a small bowl, combine cracker crumbs, egg, spices, parsley, and clams. Add sauteed vegetables. Cover and refrigerate for at least 2 hours. After chilling pour off excess liquid. Form into 6 cakes and place on a lightly oiled baking sheet. Garnish with paprika. Bake for 8-10 minutes.

Microwave *(See page 35 "Terms for Microwaving")*:
Follow above directions except: place cakes in a shallow dish. Cover and microwave on high for about 5 minutes. Pour off any moisture.

Yield: 3 servings. Calories: 149 per serving.

CLAM PIE

1 ¼ cups potatoes, peeled and sliced
    thin
¾ cup onion, thinly sliced
½ cup celery, diced
1 pint Maryland soft shell clams,
    drained and chopped, reserving
    liquid
2 ½ tablespoons flour
½ teaspoon salt
⅛ teaspoon pepper
¼ teaspoon seafood seasoning
2 tablespoons margarine
¼ cup plus 2 tablespoons clam juice
2 ½ tablespoons bacon bits
single pie crust
paprika for sprinkling

Preheat oven to 350°. Brush a pie pan lightly with oil. Layer half of the potatoes, onion and celery on the pie pan. Layer with all the clams. Sprinkle with flour and spices. Dot with margarine. Layer remaining potatoes, onion and celery and sprinkle with clam juice and bacon bits. Roll out pie crust and place over pie, flute edges. Cut slits in the crust and sprinkle with paprika. Bake for about 50 minutes. Let sit for 5 minutes to set before serving.

Yield: 4 servings. Calories: 412 per serving.

BLUEFISH

Bluefish is a voracious and compulsive eater. It gives the sportfisherman a real fight before being landed. Bluefish appear along the Atlantic and Gulf coasts from Maine to Texas. They are found world-wide in temperate continental shelf waters.

The warm waters of the Chesapeake Bay attract the Bluefish during the spring. After entering, they migrate to spawn on the outer shelf and return to the bay again in late summer.

The migratory pattern of the fish indicates its heavy activity and muscle development. The Bluefish is a dark-meat fish with a light to moderate flavor. It has a slightly higher fat content than most lean fish.

Like any fresh fish, Bluefish should have a slight ocean odor when purchased. The eyes should be clear and bright and not sunken in. The skin should be shiny and scales should stay intact. The inside cavity, once gutted, should be pink. A fresh fish should not leave an indentation when you press your finger into it.

Fresh fish may be purchased in the following manner:

Whole: Fish as they come from the water.

Drawn: Whole fish with insides removed. Generally scaled just before cooking, and usually the head, tail and fins removed at that time.

Dressed: Fish with scales and entrails removed; usually the head, tail, and fins are also removed.

Fillets: Fillets are the sides of the fish cut length-wise away from the backbone.

Butterfly-Fillets: The two sides of the fish cut length-wise away from the backbone and held together by the uncut flesh and skin of the belly.

Steaks: Steaks are cross section slices from large dressed fish.

One of the most important factors in cooking fish is to avoid overcooking it.

Bluefish is an excellent fish to barbecue. Its fine flavor is enhanced by this method. Smoking and poaching of Bluefish are two other successful methods of cooking. Small pan size blues may be fried; they have a very tender texture.

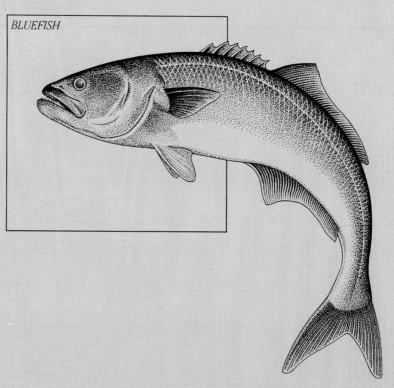

BLUEFISH

THE MANY METHODS OF FISH COOKERY

Fish is truly an amazing food. It is highly nutritious. It cooks quickly, which makes it a natural convenience food, and it is very versatile. There are several ways to cook fish.

Bake–Fish is placed on an oiled baking dish and baked in a moderate oven (350°F) until done. Fillets and steaks as well as whole fish can be baked easily. Whole fish can be stuffed prior to baking. Baking a fish with its head and tail still attached keeps it moist, and they can be removed before serving if desired.

Broil–Fish is arranged in a single layer on a well greased broiler rack, about 4 inches away from the heat source. Fish can be basted before, during and after broiling. It is not necessary to turn the fish.

Pan Fry–Fish is dipped into milk or beaten egg and then into bread crumbs, flour or your favorite dredging mix; 1/4" to 1/2" of oil is heated in a skillet and the fish placed in the hot oil in a single layer. It is turned once midway during cooking.

Oven Fry–Fish is prepared as in pan frying and is then placed on an oiled or greased shallow baking dish. It is baked in a very hot oven (500°F). It is not necessary to turn or baste the fish. Follow the 10 minute rule. (See Cooking Times Section.)

Deep Fat Fry–Prepare fish as in pan frying. Place a single layer of fish in a wire frying basket. Heat oil to 375°F in a fryer or deep fry pan. Lower the basket into the oil gently to prevent excess bubbling. Fish is fried until lightly browned, about 3-5 minutes. It should flake easily but remain moist when done. Drain on paper towels.

Poach–Fish is placed in a wide, shallow pan or dish. Liquid is added to barely cover the single layer of fish. Milk, wine, lemon water are just a few liquids that can be used. Liquid is brought to a boil, then heat is reduced and fish is simmered until done.

Steam–A steam cooker or roasting pan with a tight cover is used. The pot should be deep enough to hold a wire basket or rack to keep the fish above the liquid. About 2 inches of water is poured into the pot and brought to a boil. Fish is placed in a basket or on a rack over the liquid. The pot is covered tightly and the fish is steamed until done.

Plank–A plank or board is oiled and heated slowly in the oven. Fish is then arranged on the plank, brushed with margarine or butter and baked in a 350°F oven. Use whole fish, steaks or fillets.

Barbecue–Select a barbecue with a closely spaced grill. Grill should be well greased. Place fish on grill 4 inches from hot coals. Baste with a sauce if desired. Turn half way through cooking. Foil may also be used, but poke holes in it to help circulate the heat. Fish must be watched closely as it cooks very fast.

Microwave–Fish cooked in the microwave is tender, moist and flavorful. Seafood is naturally very delicate. It is less dense than red meat and cooks much faster. Because of oven variations, some experimenting may be necessary to find the correct cooking time for your oven.

Fillets can usually be cooked at high power. However, some ovens may produce ''popping'' more than others. If popping occurs, it is best to cook the fish at medium power or 50%. Three minutes a pound of boneless fish is a general guide although this varies with the thickness. Thick steaks should be turned halfway through cooking time.

If a sauce is to be cooked over the fish in the same dish, 80% power level should be used, and the cooking time increased as necessary.

TIPS FOR MICROWAVING

1. Use a shallow baking dish, preferably flat so that the fish gets maximum exposure to the microwaves.

2. Cover the fish with plastic wrap and vent by turning back one corner during cooking.

3. Keep fish covered with plastic for 5 minutes after removing from oven. This allows fish to continue cooking in the center and remain moist around the edges.

4. If fish is to be served with rice or vegetables, cook the rice or vegetables first and keep them covered while cooking the fish. The rice or vegetables will retain heat longer than the fish.

5. Rotate fish as necessary during microwaving to ensure even cooking.

TERMS FOR MICROWAVING

Although there are many different microwave ovens on the market today, below is a listing of the appropriate temperature definitions used in this cookbook.

High–most power–fastest cooking
Roast or Medium–medium energy–slightly lower than high
Simmer–slow and gentle cooking–mid-heat range
Warm–gentlest in power

COOKING TIMES

Proper timing is the secret to cooking fish and other seafood. Fish is done when the flesh becomes opaque or white, firm, but still remains moist. To cook until the fish becomes flaky may overcook it and the meat will become tough and dry.

As a general rule for cooking times, measure the fish fillet or steak at its thickest part. Allow ten minutes of cooking for each inch. For frozen fish, the cooking time should be doubled (20 minutes for each inch). If the fish is cooked in foil or sauce, allow an extra five minutes for each inch. Test for doneness during preparation to avoid overcooking.

SHARK

Eating shark sounds like an act of revenge, but shark is a surprisingly delicious food that is considered excellent eating in many parts of the world. It is nutritious, economical, low in fat, firm in texture, mild in flavor, the fillets lack bones and the Spiny Dogfish species has an eye-appealing lean white meat.

Shark is versatile. It is an excellent fish for grilling, broiling, poaching, baking, frying and kabobs. It has a very mild flavor, somewhat like flounder or trout.

Approximately 62 species of sharks inhabit the eastern waters of North America. Many are oceanic and roam the high seas, while others live close to the

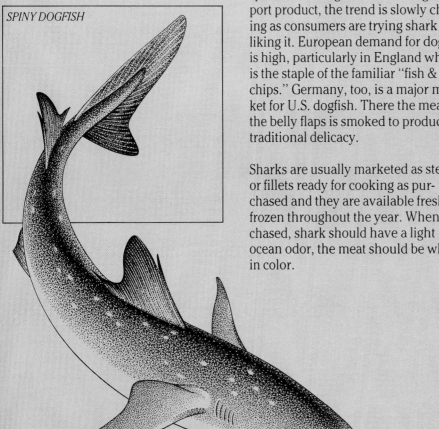

SPINY DOGFISH

bottom. The majority stay in comparatively shallow water. Sharks that are commonly caught in the estuarine and inshore areas along the Mid-Atlantic coast are usually three to seven feet in length and under 1,000 pounds, although larger ones do exist.

One of the most abundant sharks, the Spiny Dogfish, is very plentiful in the Mid-Atlantic region of the East Coast. This is a relatively small shark averaging 3 to 4 feet in length. The season for shark is somewhat sporadic. They are usually in Mid-Atlantic waters in November, December, January, March and April.

Consumers are slowly accepting shark as an economical alternative to other species. Although shark is a large export product, the trend is slowly changing as consumers are trying shark and liking it. European demand for dogfish is high, particularly in England where it is the staple of the familiar "fish & chips." Germany, too, is a major market for U.S. dogfish. There the meat of the belly flaps is smoked to produce a traditional delicacy.

Sharks are usually marketed as steaks or fillets ready for cooking as purchased and they are available fresh or frozen throughout the year. When purchased, shark should have a light ocean odor, the meat should be white in color.

Most shark purchased from a retailer has been properly handled by the processor. However, if you want to prepare a fish that you have just caught, it should be soaked in 1/2 tablespoon lemon juice or 1 tablespoon of cider vinegar for each pound of fish and just enough ice water to cover the fish. Refrigerate for at least 4 hours. This will neutralize any ammonia that may be present. An alternate method is to soak the shark in an icy solution of 1 cup salt dissolved in 1 gallon of water.

To prepare a freshly caught shark for cooking, grasp it by tail, belly side down and cut along the top side from the tail to the back of the head. Turn the shark over and repeat on the belly side. Hold shark belly-side down and make cuts perpendicular to the first cut on both sides of the head. Grasp the skin at the back of the head and remove with a sharp knife. After skinning, place shark belly-side up. Pull head and viscera from body cavity and cut off tail. Wash cavity thoroughly and fillet.

Plan to prepare fresh shark as soon as possible. If the meat is to be stored longer than 24 hours, it should be kept in an air tight container in the freezer.

Photo opposite: Baked Stuffed Bluefish

1 3-pound bluefish, scaled and gutted
¼ teaspoon salt
⅛ teaspoon pepper
1 ½ teaspoons lemon juice

Stuffing:
1 ½ cups fresh mushrooms, sliced
½ teaspoon pimento, chopped and
    drained
¼ cup plus 2 tablespoons celery,
    chopped
¼ cup onions, diced
2 teaspoons olive oil
2 tablespoons seasoned bread crumbs
½ teaspoon seafood seasoning
lemon and mushroom slices for garnish
paprika

Sprinkle inside of fish with salt, pepper, and lemon juice. Saute vegetables in 2 teaspoons oil for 5-7 minutes. Drain and add seasonings and bread crumbs. Stuff fish. Close and garnish top with lemon and mushroom slices. Sprinkle with paprika. Bake approximately 25 minutes at 350°F. Check fish for doneness with a fork inserted in thickest part, fish should be firm but still moist.

Yield: 4 servings. Calories: 206 per serving.

2 pounds bluefish fillets, cut in strips
    7″ long, 1″ wide

Sauce:
¼ cup plus ½ tablespoon
    margarine
¼ cup plus 2 ½ tablespoons flour
⅓ teaspoon white pepper
¾ teaspoon onion salt
¼ cup plus 2 tablespoons sherry
2 ¼ cups skim milk
3 tablespoons dried parsley
paprika for garnish
lemon slices for garnish

Conventional oven:
Preheat oven to 425°F. Roll up fillets (from tail end to head end) to form turbans. Place on a baking dish. In a small sauce pan, melt margarine over medium-low heat. Blend in flour and stir until bubbly. Add remaining sauce ingredients and cook, stirring often, until slightly thickened. Spoon sauce over each fillet, just enough to cover the top and sides. Sprinkle with paprika and bake for 10-12 minutes, until fish is moist and flaky. Serve roll-ups on a bed of rice or make individual servings by placing 2 roll-ups in scalloped shells. Garnish with lemon slices.

Microwave *(See page 35 "Terms for Microwaving")*:
Place roll-ups in 2 baking dishes (1 pound in each). Place margarine in a small bowl and microwave on roast for 2 minutes. Blend in flour. Stir in remaining sauce ingredients and microwave on roast for 2 minutes. Spoon sauce over fillets and cover dish with plastic. Microwave one dish (1 pound) at a time for about 8 minutes on roast.

Yield: 6 servings. Calories: 343 per serving.

CHARCOAL GRILLED BLUEFISH

2 pounds bluefish fillets, skin removed
2 cups Italian dressing
2 lemons, cut in wedges

(can use lowfat Italian dressing)

Place bluefish fillets in a baking dish. Pour dressing over fillets, cover and refrigerate for 2 hours. Place fillets on a hot, oiled grill. Baste fillets frequently with dressing and cook for about 10 minutes. Turn and baste again. Fillets are done when firm and still juicy. Serve with fresh sliced lemon. For ease in cooking, cover grill with foil and poke holes in it to circulate heat.

Yield: 6 servings. Calories: 184 per serving.

DILLED BLUEFISH

1½ pounds bluefish fillets
   (4 fillets—¾" thick)
⅓ cup green onion, chopped
1 teaspoon instant chicken bouillon
1 cup water
2 teaspoons lemon juice
pinch salt
⅛–¼ teaspoon pepper

Sauce:
2 teaspoons margarine
2 teaspoons flour
pinch salt
½ teaspoon dill weed
½ cup yogurt, lowfat plain
¼ cup plus 2 tablespoons fish
liquor (from baking dish)
lemon wedges

Arrange fillets in a baking dish, thickest pieces toward outside. Sprinkle fillets with green onion. In a small bowl, mix together chicken bouillon, water, lemon juice, salt and pepper. Pour mixture over fillets.

Conventional oven:
Bake in a 425° preheated oven for 10-12 minutes. Mix together sauce ingredients (using fish liquid from baking dish for the fish liquor) in a small sauce pan. Heat over medium low. Serve sauce over fish. Garnish with lemon.

Microwave *(See page 35 "Terms for Microwaving")*:
Cover dish with plastic and microwave for 7 minutes on high. Uncover and test fish to see if it flakes (microwave 1 more minute on high if necessary). Let stand 5 minutes. Prepare dill sauce by combining all sauce ingredients in a small bowl and microwave on roast for 2 minutes. Stir and microwave for 3 more minutes. Serve over fish, garnish with lemon slices.

Yield: 4 servings. Calories: 287 per serving.

CORA'S FISH CAKES

2 pounds bluefish fillets
2 cups mashed potatoes
2 large eggs, beaten
2 tablespoons onion, grated
2 tablespoons chives
2 teaspoons worcestershire sauce
1 teaspoon lemon pepper
1 teaspoon salt
3 tablespoons oil, for frying

Poach fillets in a small amount of water until fish flakes easily with a fork. Remove dark meat and skin. In a small bowl, combine all other ingredients, except oil. Gently fold in flaked fish fillets. Mold into 12 cakes. Heat 1½ tablespoons oil in a large skillet. Cook 6 cakes in oil over medium heat until they turn golden brown, turning once. Drain on paper towels. Add remaining 1½ tablespoons oil to cook other cakes.

Yield: 6 servings. Calories: 285 per serving.

2 pounds bluefish fillets
¾ teaspoon salt
⅛ teaspoon pepper
4 green onions, chopped
1 teaspoon margarine
¼ cup Italian bread crumbs
2½ teaspoons lemon juice

Lemon Sauce:
½ cup margarine, melted
2 tablespoons plus 2 teaspoons lemon
  juice
⅛ teaspoon beau monde

Conventional oven:
Preheat oven to 400°. Place fillets on a lightly oiled baking sheet or shallow casserole dish. Sprinkle with salt, pepper and onion. Dot with margarine. Cover with bread crumbs, then sprinkle with lemon juice and paprika. Bake for about 10-12 minutes.

Microwave *(See page 35 "Terms for Microwaving")*:
Follow same procedure except cover and microwave on high for about 7 minutes. Allow to stand for 5 minutes then test for doneness. Serve with lemon sauce.

Yield: 6 servings. Calories: 204 per serving. 69 calories per tablespoon lemon sauce.

---

2 pounds bluefish fillets, cut into
  12 strips
1 cup white wine
¾ teaspoon salt
½ teaspoon lemon pepper
1 teaspoon oregano
½ cup parsley, finely chopped
½ cup almonds, crushed
12 cherry tomatoes
3 cups cooked medium egg noodles
¼ cup fresh parsley, finely chopped
¼ cup romano cheese
1 tablespoon olive oil
pinch lemon pepper

Conventional oven:
Preheat oven to 400°F. Soak fish strips in wine for 5 to 10 minutes in the refrigerator. In a small bowl, mix together spices, parsley, and almonds. Dip fish strips in mixture, then roll each piece around a cherry tomato. Place rolls on a lightly oiled baking dish. Bake for 10 to 14 minutes. While fish is baking, prepare noodles according to package directions. Drain and add parsley, cheese, oil and pepper. Place fish rolls on bed of noodles and serve immediately.

Microwave *(See page 35 "Terms for Microwaving")*:
Follow procedure for conventional method. Place fish rolls in a microwave dish, cover with plastic and microwave for about 6-7 minutes on high. Let stand covered for 5 minutes. Serve over a bed of noodles.

Yield: 6 servings. Calories: 401 per serving (including ½ cup noodles).

1 pound bluefish fillets, cut in 1″ chunks
2 tablespoons lemon juice
¼ teaspoon salt
¼ teaspoon pepper
½ cup water
⅓ cup lemon juice
2 large tomatoes, sliced and quartered
⅔ cup celery, sliced diagonally
1 16-ounce can artichoke hearts, sliced
2 medium green peppers, cut in short
   strips
⅔ cup water chestnuts, sliced thin
⅔ cup cucumber, thinly sliced
2 tablespoons sunflower seeds
⅔ cup carrots, cut into long, thin
   slivers using a peeler
1 head lettuce

Lemon Dressing:
⅓ cup lemon juice
⅓ cup plus 1 tablespoon salad oil
⅛ teaspoon pepper
⅛ teaspoon salt
¾ teaspoon sugar
1 teaspoon chives

Place bluefish chunks in a small bowl. Pour lemon juice, salt and pepper over fish, stir and cover. Refrigerate for at least one hour. After one hour, drain fish. Place chunks in a skillet and add ½ cup water and ⅓ cup lemon juice to the fish. Cover and simmer over medium heat for about 7-8 minutes or until fish is flaky and moist. Remove from heat and store covered, in the refrigerator, until ready to serve the salad. In a large bowl, combine remaining ingredients. Toss well. When fish is chilled, lightly toss in chunks. Serve with lemon dressing.

Yield: 4 servings. Calories: 236 per serving. 68 per tablespoon of dressing.

SHARK KABOBS

1 pound shark fillets, cut in 1″ cubes
8 cherry tomatoes, whole
1 cup zucchini, cut in ½″ slices
1 cup green pepper, cut in small pieces
8 mushrooms, whole
1 cup onion, cut in small pieces
½ cup Italian dressing

Place chunks of fish and vegetables on 8-10″ long skewers (each skewer will have 3 pieces of fish). Place skewers in a shallow dish and pour Italian dressing evenly over kabobs. Cover and marinate in the refrigerator for 1 hour, turn after ½ hour. Oil grill. Place kabobs on hot grill and cook for about 15 minutes basting 2 or 3 times with the dressing. Turn often to ensure even cooking. Kabobs are done when fish is firm. Serve 2 kabobs per person.

Yield: 4 servings. Calories: 298 per serving.

SHARK IN CUCUMBER SAUCE

Cucumber sauce:
2 tablespoons margarine
1 medium cucumber, peeled, quartered,
    sliced
4 scallions, chopped
2 tablespoons fresh parsley, chopped
2 tablespoons cornstarch
2 cups skim milk
1 ½ teaspoons instant chicken
    bouillon
¼ teaspoon onion powder
½ teaspoon lemon pepper
¾ teaspoon sage
1 tablespoon lemon juice

1 pound shark fillets, cut into round
    chunks (using a donut hole cutter)
½ teaspoon salt
1 tablespoon lemon juice
2 teaspoons margarine
2 tablespoons pimento, chopped
2 lemons, sliced
3 cups cooked long grain and wild rice

Preheat oven to 400°F. To make sauce, melt margarine in a medium sauce pan. Add cucumber, scallions and parsley and saute for 5 minutes. Add cornstarch and mix well. Stir in milk. Add chicken bouillon, spices, and lemon juice. Cook over medium heat until sauce comes to a boil, stirring often, about 20 minutes. While sauce is cooking, place shark in a baking dish and sprinkle with salt, lemon juice and margarine. Cover and bake for 10 minutes. Measure out 1 cup of cooked sauce and stir into cooked rice. Spoon rice onto a large serving dish. Arrange shark over bed of rice, then top with sauce. Sprinkle with chopped pimento, garnish with lemon slices.

Yield: 4 servings. Calories: 463 per serving.

¾ cup white wine
3 tablespoons lemon juice
1 tablespoon worcestershire sauce
2 pounds shark fillets, cut in 2″ x 1″
   pieces
⅔ cup walnuts, very finely chopped
¼ cup onion, minced
⅔ cup celery, minced
¼ cup dried parsley
¼ cup bread crumbs
¼ teaspoon seafood seasoning
¼ teaspoon salt
⅛ teaspoon lemon pepper
paprika for garnish
2 10-ounce packages frozen snow peas
   (pea pods)

Conventional oven:
Preheat oven to 400°F. Mix together wine, lemon juice and worcestershire sauce. Place fillets in a shallow dish and pour mixture evenly over fish. Marinate fish in refrigerator for ½ hour. In a medium bowl, combine walnuts, onion, celery, parsley, bread crumbs and seasonings. Spread a thin layer of walnuts mixture over each fillet. Sprinkle with paprika. Discard marinade. To bake, place fillets on a lightly oiled (2 teaspoons) baking pan and bake for 10-15 minutes until fish is flaky and moist. While fish is baking, place frozen pea pods in a sauce pan with ½ cup water. Add salt and pepper to taste. Cook just until hot. Do not overcook. Serve fish on a bed of pea pods.

Microwave *(See page 35 "Terms for Microwaving")*:
Follow above directions, instead of baking, place fillets in a shallow dish, cover with plastic and microwave 7-8 minutes on high. Remove and allow to stand 5 minutes covered to finish cooking. While fish is standing, microwave frozen pea pods in a dish for 5 minutes on high.

Yield: 6 servings. Calories: 368 per serving.

POACHED SHARK IN SHERRY

2 pounds shark fillets, cut into 8 pieces, ¾" thick
1 tablespoon margarine
¼ cup mushrooms, sliced
¼ cup onions, sliced
¼ cup green pepper, cut in thin strips
¾ cup sherry
¼ teaspoon lemon juice
⅛ teaspoon each—salt, sage, thyme, white pepper
Parsley and paprika for sprinkling
Lemon slices, halved, for garnish

Conventional oven:
Preheat oven to 425°F. In a skillet, melt margarine and saute mushrooms, onions and peppers for 3-4 minutes until slightly soft. Arrange fish in a 9 x 12 casserole dish. Sprinkle vegetables over fish. Combine the sherry, lemon juice and spices and pour this mixture over vegetables. Sprinkle with parsley and paprika. Bake for 20 minutes. Serve with lemon slices.

Microwave *(See page 35 "Terms for Microwaving")*:
Place margarine in a glass baking dish. Microwave on roast for 1½ minutes. Add vegetables to margarine and microwave for 2 minutes on simmer. Push vegetables to the side. Arrange fish in the same dish placing thickest pieces toward the outside. Sprinkle vegetables over fish. Combine sherry, lemon juice and spices. Pour over vegetables. Sprinkle with parsley and paprika. Cover with plastic. Microwave 7 minutes on medium heat. Rotate dish and microwave 7 more minutes on medium. Allow more time for thicker fillets.

Yield: 6 servings. Calories: 294 per serving.

BARBECUED SHARK

Sauce:
1 cup vinegar
2 cups ketchup
¼ teaspoon each onion powder, garlic powder, nutmeg
½ teaspoon dry mustard
1⅓ teaspoons hot chili sauce
2 tablespoons sweet relish
3 tablespoons brown sugar
1 teaspoon horseradish
⅛ teaspoon pepper
2 tablespoons fresh parsley, finely chopped

2 pounds shark fillets

In a medium bowl, combine all sauce ingredients and mix well. Oil grill and heat. Arrange shark fillets on hot grill a few at a time. Baste with barbecue sauce. Turn after 5 minutes. Baste other side with sauce and cook until fish is flaky and moist, about 10 minutes.

Yield: 6 servings. Calories: 354 per serving.

SWEET AND SOUR SHARK

2 pounds fresh shark, cut in 2″ chunks
3 tablespoons vegetable oil
1 20-ounce can pineapple chunks, packed in own juice
1¼ cups pineapple juice plus water
¼ cup cider vinegar
¼ cup brown sugar, packed
3 tablespoons cornstarch
1 tablespoon soy sauce
1 teaspoon salt
½ teaspoon garlic salt
1 8-ounce can water chestnuts, sliced thin
1 cup green pepper, cut in small squares
1 cup tomato, cut in thin wedges

6 cups cooked long grain rice

Conventional oven:
Saute shark in oil for 5 minutes in a large skillet. Drain pineapple and pour juice into a 2 cup measuring glass. Add water to make 1¼ cup of liquid. Mix liquid with cider vinegar, brown sugar, cornstarch, soy sauce, and salts. Pour this mixture over fish in skillet and stir for about 3 minutes over medium heat. Transfer fish to a small bowl. Add pineapple, water chestnuts, green pepper and tomato to skillet and cook over medium high heat until vegetables are hot and slightly tender, about 8 minutes. Add fish and cook until done, about 4 more minutes. Serve over rice with soy sauce or mustard sauce.

Microwave *(See page 35 "Terms for Microwaving")*:
Place shark pieces in a baking dish with thickest pieces to the outside. Drain pineapple and pour juice into a 2 cup measuring glass and add water if necessary to make ¾ cup of liquid. Add remaining sauce ingredients, mix well, and pour over shark. Sprinkle chestnuts, green pepper and pineapple over shark. Stir gently and cover with plastic. Microwave on high for 10 minutes. Stir in tomato and microwave on high for 2 minutes. Allow to stand covered for 5 minutes before serving. Microwave longer if necessary to thicken sauce.

Yield: 6 servings. Calories: 595 per serving (conventional), 535 per serving (microwave).

SHARK A L'ORANGE

2 pounds shark fillets, cut into 4″ pieces
¼ teaspoon celery salt
¼ teaspoon pepper
2 cups orange juice
2 tablespoons plus 2 teaspoons lemon juice
¾ teaspoon nutmeg
1 tablespoon cornstarch
¼ teaspoon salt and pepper
½ cup walnuts, chopped
2 teaspoons oil for baking pan
2 whole oranges, sliced
paprika and parsley for garnish

Conventional oven:
Place shark fillets in a shallow baking dish. Sprinkle with celery salt and pepper. In a small bowl, mix together juices, nutmeg, cornstarch, salt, pepper and walnuts. Pour mixture over fillets, cover and refrigerate for 30-40 minutes. Preheat broiler 10-15 minutes before cooking. Arrange fillets on a lightly oiled baking pan. Baste with orange sauce. Broil for about 7 minutes, or until fish flakes easily. While fish is broiling, heat remaining sauce in a small sauce pan over medium heat until hot. When fish is done, arrange on a serving plate with orange slices. Sprinkle fillets lightly with paprika and garnish with parsley. Serve sauce on the side.

Microwave *(See page 35 "Terms for Microwaving")*:
Follow above directions except for broiling fillets. Arrange drained fillets in 2 microwave dishes, thickest pieces on the outside of the dish. Cover with plastic and microwave one dish (1 pound) at a time for 5 minutes on high. Fish is cooked when firm and moist. Microwave longer if necessary. Repeat for second pound.

Yield: 6 servings. Calories: 337 per serving.

SHARK WITH CAPER SAUCE

Sauce:
3 tablespoons whole capers
1 cup white wine
1 tablespoon lemon juice
¼ cup margarine
½ teaspoon each salt, pepper
3 teaspoons cornstarch
3 tablespoons celery, minced
1 tablespoon dried parsley
1 tablespoon Dijon mustard

2 pounds shark fillets
parsley for garnish
lemon wedges

Conventional oven:
Mix together sauce ingredients in a small sauce pan and cook for 3 minutes on medium high heat until thick. Stir well. Place fillets in a small dish. Cover with ¼ cup sauce. Refrigerate for 30 minutes. Preheat oven to 400°. Transfer fillets to a baking dish and bake for 10 minutes. While fish is baking, heat remaining sauce over low until hot. Serve sauce over fish with parsley and lemon.

Microwave *(See page 35 "Terms for Microwaving")*:
Mix together sauce ingredients in a small glass bowl. Cover and microwave on high for 2 minutes. Stir well. Marinate fish with ¼ cup sauce in refrigerator for 30 minutes. Transfer fish to a baking dish, cover and microwave on high for 8 minutes. Allow fish to stand covered while the sauce is being microwaved on roast for 2 more minutes to finish cooking. Serve sauce over fish with parsley and lemon.

Yield: 6 servings. Calories: 350 per serving.

SHARK EN PAPILLOTE

¼ cup margarine
½ cup green pepper, diced
2 ounces canned mushrooms, sliced
¼ cup flour
1 teaspoon salt
1 teaspoon dry mustard
dash cayenne pepper
2 cups skim milk
2 pounds shark fillets, ½″ thick
1 pound Maryland regular or
**   backfin crabmeat, picked**
**   of cartilage**
paprika for garnish

Preheat oven to 375°F. Melt margarine in a large sauce pan. Saute green pepper and mushrooms in margarine for 5 minutes. In a small bowl, combine flour, salt, mustard and pepper. Gradually blend flour mixture into margarine. Add milk slowly and stir constantly over medium heat until mixture thickens. Set aside. Prepare aluminum foil for papillote by cutting 6-12 x 16 inch sheets of foil. Fold each sheet in half and cut in the shape of a folded heart. Unfold and lightly oil one side. Place a fillet on the oiled side of each foil. Pour sauce over each fillet. Sprinkle fillets with 1/6 of the crabmeat, then sprinkle with paprika. Close up foil and fold sides. Poke 4 or 5 small holes in bottom of foil. Place on a baking sheet in the oven for 25-30 minutes. Test for doneness. May be served in or out of foil package.

Yield: 6 servings. Calories: 429 per serving.

SHARK TERIYAKI

¼ cup soy sauce
½ cup sherry
1 tablespoon sugar
1 garlic clove, minced
½ teaspoon ground ginger
⅛ teaspoon white pepper
2 pounds shark fillets
lemon slices for garnish

In a small sauce pan, combine soy sauce, sherry, sugar, garlic, ginger and pepper. Cook over medium heat until sauce boils. Arrange shark fillets in a shallow baking dish. Pour sauce over shark. Cover and refrigerate for 30 minutes. Place fillets on a hot grill and cook until fish is firm and moist, about 10-15 minutes. Serve with lemon slices.

Yield: 6 servings. Calories: 281 per serving.

SCALLOPS

There are basically two kinds of scallops of commercial importance to consumers. The Bay Scallop is a small scallop with an "eye" measuring one half inch across. It is taken from inshore bays and estuaries from New England to the Gulf of Mexico. It is a shallow water scallop.

The Sea Scallop is a deep water scallop and is harvested from the deep waters off the Northern and Middle Atlantic States. Its "eye" measures up to two inches in diameter.

The scallop may vary in color from white to gray or bluish. Only the adductor muscle or "eye," which opens and closes the shell, is consumed by Americans. Europeans eat the entire scallop. Scallops are usually shucked on board the boat, and the "eye" removed. Scallop fishing is seasonal since most states enforce a closed season, April to October, to protect the scallops from being overfished.

Scallop meat is marketed fresh in 12 and 14 ounce cartons in chilled display cases. Frozen scallops, both raw and precooked, are also marketed and are usually breaded.

When purchasing fresh sea scallops, the meat should be white, the Bay Scallop should be creamy white, light tan or pinkish. The meat should be firm and have a sweetish odor.

Sea scallops are excellent when used for seafood kabobs because of their size and firm texture.

ROE

Shad, from the Mid-Atlantic region, is a very popular species of fish that contains roe ranging in size from three to ten ounces. They are generally sold in pairs; small roe is three to four ounces, medium is four to six ounces, and large is eight to ten ounces. Jumbo roe may also be purchased as the shad migrates farther north and grows in size.

One of the most common methods of preparation is to remove the egg sacs from the fish whole, wash carefully, and simply fry in a small amount of fat or oil.

Fish roe are an excellent source of protein but tend to be high in both fat and cholesterol. Some other Mid-Atlantic species of fish that contain edible roe are herring, mullet and rockfish.

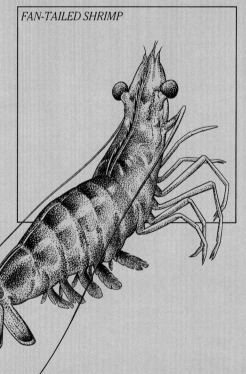

FAN-TAILED SHRIMP

SHRIMP

Live shrimp come in a variety of pale colors, pink, brown, white or gray, but they all turn pink after cooking. Shrimp are fished commercially along the Atlantic Coast from Virginia to Brazil and in the Gulf of Mexico.

White shrimp, pink shrimp and brown shrimp are the most popular species. White shrimp are the common greenish gray shrimp found in the shallow waters of bays and other inshore areas. The brown shrimp is brownish-red in its raw state and the pink shrimp is pink or coral.

The yield from whole shrimp is approximately fifty percent. Shrimp are available either raw or cooked, peeled or unpeeled, and fresh or frozen. Shrimp are termed "whole" if they consist of five or more segments of shrimp flesh.

When purchased fresh shrimp should have a mild odor and firm meat. The meat and shells should not be slippery.

Shrimp are customarily sold according to size or grade, based on the number of heads-off shrimp to the pound. The largest size or grade runs fifteen or fewer to the pound, the smallest runs sixty or more to the pound. Most shrimp are sold by count ranges of five rather than grade. Common counts are 16-20, 21-25 and 26-30 shrimp per pound.

Shrimp take very little time to cook. If frozen, thaw out the shrimp and steam them only three to five minutes. When cooked, shrimp should be tender, not tough which overcooking will do. Frozen shrimp should be thawed to ensure even cooking.

LOBSTER

Lobsters, of which there are more than 200 species, range in color from light green to deep blue. The large muscle of the tail is prized for its flavor.

The two most important species are the Northern Lobster and the Spiny Lobster. The Northern Lobster is most often referred to as the "Maine Lobster" because it is primarily produced there. The "Spiny" or "Rock" lobsters are related to lobsters but are actually sea crawfish. Spiny lobsters do not have the large heavy claws of the true lobster. They are caught off the coast of Florida.

Lobsters may be purchased in several forms. Live, whole cooked in the shell, frozen, and canned cooked meat are just a few of the forms. Live lobsters missing one claw are marketed as "pistols." Those missing both claws are marketed as "culls."

Lobsters should be alive when purchased. They should show movement in the legs and tail when touched. Cooked lobsters should show a bright red color when cooked, whether they are green or brown to start with. They should have a light seashore odor.

SQUID

Squid belongs to the class of mollusks known as cephalopods. Unlike other mollusks such as oysters, clams and scallops, squid have a compact internal shell or quill sometimes referred to as the pen. They have no outer shell.

Squid (calamari) ordinarily have a milky, translucent appearance, but have the ability to change color. An ink-like fluid is contained in a sac in the squid's mantle. This fluid is used as a defense mechanism which is ejected to aid in escape from enemies.

Squid have been popular as a food in Europe and Asia for centuries. It is high in protein and contains phosphorus, calcium, thiamin and riboflavin.

Whole squid is available on the market fresh or frozen. Canned squid is commercially prepared with or without its ink in brine, in oil, or in tomato sauce. Fresh and thawed frozen squid should smell clean and fresh, the skin of fresh squid should be creamy in color with red flecks. As the squid begins to spoil, pigments are released into the flesh, causing an apparent change in the color of the skin.

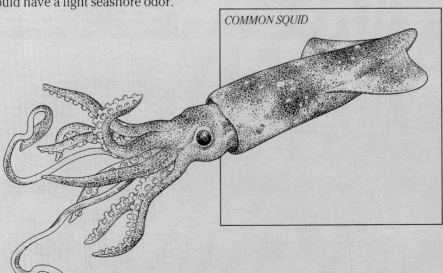

COMMON SQUID

EEL

The American eel is a true fish, having gills, fins and other parts that are characteristics of fish such as trout, bass and perch. Its snake-like appearance has unfortunately hampered its acceptability as a food fish, but only in this country. In most other countries, eel is regarded as a delicacy.

Eels are found in abundance from Greenland to the Gulf of Mexico. In Maryland, eels are found in freshwater creeks, ponds, rivers, brackish tidewaters, and coastal bays. No other species in Maryland thrives in such a wide range of environments. Eels constitute a significant percentage of the total fish population in Maryland and represent a tremendous natural resource.

Once the eel has been skinned, a dark skin-like membrane is apparent. This membrane should be removed from the eel before cooking because it distracts from the good flavor of the eel. Here is one way to remove the membrane:

Cut the whole, skinned eel in half. Bring about 4 cups of water to boiling in a large sauce pan. Using tongs, quickly dip half the eel in the boiling water. The eel shouldn't be blanched for more than 5 or 6 seconds. Lay eel on a cutting board and quickly scrape off the membrane with a sharp knife. Now the eel is ready to fillet.

Eel has a rather mild, distinct flavor. It is quite tasty when cooked properly but can become tough if overcooked. Eel can be frozen in home freezers. Be sure to wrap them air tight with freezer wrap and store no longer than three months.

BOUILLABAISSE

2 large garlic cloves, crushed
½ cup celery, chopped
½ cup onion, chopped
½ cup green pepper, chopped
¼ cup olive oil
2 bay leaves
½ tablespoon oregano
¼ cup fresh parsley, chopped
½ teaspoon crushed red pepper
1 teaspoon salt
24 ounces canned tomatoes, chopped
4 ounces clam juice
2 cups water
½ cup sherry
½ pound shrimp, cleaned, medium
1 pint Maryland standard oysters,
  shucked
½ pound white fish fillets, cut
  into chunks
½ pound Maryland regular crabmeat,
  cartilage removed
6 Littleneck clams, scrubbed
6 mussels, scrubbed
½ pound squid, cleaned,
  cut in 1″ squares

In a large 4 quart pot, saute garlic, celery, onion and green pepper in oil until tender. Add spices and tomatoes. Simmer for 1 hour. Add clam juice, water and sherry and simmer for 10 minutes. Add shrimp, oysters and fish and simmer about 3 minutes. Add crabmeat, clams, mussels and squid. Simmer until clams and mussels open. Serve immediately.

Yield: 6 servings. Calories: 300 per serving.

SEAFOOD CASSEROLE

½ tablespoon margarine
½ pound shrimp, peeled, deveined
½ pound lobster meat or scallops
1 clove garlic, minced
¼ cup green pepper, diced
¼ cup white wine
1 teaspoon lemon juice
1 egg, beaten
¼ cup low calorie mayonnaise
1 teaspoon dry mustard
½ teaspoon salt
¼ teaspoon seafood seasoning
⅛ teaspoon pepper
1 pound Maryland backfin crabmeat,
  cartilage removed
¼ cup seasoned bread crumbs
¼ cup cheddar cheese, grated
paprika for sprinkling

Preheat oven to 400°F. Melt margarine in a skillet and add shrimp, lobster, garlic and green pepper. Saute for 5 minutes. Transfer contents of skillet to a casserole dish. In a small bowl, mix together wine, lemon juice, egg, mayonnaise, mustard and seasonings. Beat until well blended. Gently fold crabmeat and bread crumbs into liquid. Pour mixture over seafood in casserole and sprinkle with cheese and paprika. Bake for 10-12 minutes.

Yield: 4 servings. Calories: 170 per serving.

LOBSTER BISQUE

1 ½ cups water
1 chicken bouillon cube
½ cup each carrots, onions, potatoes,
    chopped
pinch white pepper
¼ teaspoon Italian seasoning
salt to taste
3 tablespoons white wine
¾ cup skim milk
½ pound lobster meat, uncooked,
    chopped

Dissolve bouillon cube in boiling water in a small sauce pan. Add chopped vegetables and simmer until tender. Pour contents of pan into blender and puree. Transfer back to sauce pan and add seasonings, wine and milk. Add lobster and cook over low heat for 20 minutes. Serve hot.

Yield: 3 cups. 6 servings, ½ cup each. Calories: 68 per serving.

JAMBALAYA

3 tablespoons margarine
¾ cup green pepper, chopped
¼ cup celery, chopped
⅓ cup onion, chopped
½ cup fresh parsley, chopped
1 16-ounce can tomatoes, chopped
2 cups water
1 ½ teaspoons chicken bouillon
½ teaspoon salt
⅛ teaspoon pepper
½ teaspoon chili powder
2 bay leaves
2 cups cooked rice
1 pint Maryland standard oysters,
    drained
½ pound white fish, cut in chunks
1 pound Maryland regular crabmeat,
    cartilage removed

Saute green pepper, celery and onion in margarine for 5 minutes in a large sauce pan. Add parsley, tomatoes, water, bouillon and seasonings and simmer over medium heat for 30-40 minutes. Add rice, oysters and fish and simmer for 10 minutes. Add crabmeat and simmer for 5 minutes.

Yield: 6 servings. Calories: 300 per serving.

SEAFOOD KABOBS

½ pound sea scallops
½ pound medium shrimp, peeled,
    deveined
½ pound flounder fillets
½ teaspoon salt
¼ teaspoon pepper

Basting sauce:
⅓ cup margarine
2 cloves garlic, minced
2 tablespoons lemon juice

Rice Pilaf:
¼ cup margarine
½ cup onion, diced
1 clove garlic, minced
1 cup long grain rice, uncooked
¼ teaspoon ground corriander
½ teaspoon cinnamon
½ teaspoon salt
⅛ teaspoon pepper
2½ cups water
½ cup parsley, chopped

Arrange the seafood and fish on 10″ skewers, placing 2 of each species on a skewer. Sprinkle with salt and pepper. Refrigerate until grill is hot and sauce and rice are cooked. To make basting sauce, melt margarine and add garlic and juice. To make rice, combine all ingredients except parsley in a medium sauce pan. Simmer until all water is absorbed. Add parsley and stir. Keep covered. Place skewers on hot grill and baste with sauce. Grill until done, turning as needed. Serve over rice and sprinkle with paprika.

Yield: 4 servings, 2 kabobs each. Calories: 348 per serving.

(see photo, page 42)

SEAFOOD GUMBO

Roux:
3 tablespoons margarine or salad oil
3 tablespoons flour

6 cups water
1 10-ounce package okra, thawed,
    chopped
2 cups onion, chopped
¾ cup carrots, sliced
¾ cup celery, chopped
1 16-ounce can tomatoes, chopped
1 clove garlic, minced
2 tablespoons chicken bouillon
3 bacon strips, fried, drained, crumbled
1 tablespoon lemon juice
½ teaspoon seafood seasoning
½ teaspoon oregano
¼ teaspoon ground thyme
salt and pepper to taste
½ pound medium shrimp, peeled
1 pint Maryland standard oysters
    with liquor
1 pound Maryland regular crabmeat,
    cartilage removed

In a small heavy pan, melt margarine and gradually blend in flour. Stir over medium heat until mixture turns a golden brown (about 5 minutes). Reduce heat to low and cook for 25 minutes, stirring often. In a large stew pot, heat water to boiling. Add vegetables, garlic, chicken bouillon, bacon, lemon juice, seasonings, and roux. Reduce to medium low and simmer for about 45 minutes uncovered, stirring occasionally. Add shrimp and oysters and simmer for 5 minutes. Add crabmeat and simmer 5 minutes. Serve immediately. Serve with rice if desired.

Yield: 6 servings. Calories: 302 per serving.

SHAD ROE

8 strips bacon
1 medium onion
2 pair small shad roe
2 tablespoons lemon juice
3 tablespoons flour
¼ teaspoon each salt, lemon pepper
⅛ teaspoon each garlic powder, onion
   powder, fine herbs
parsley for sprinkling
lemon slices

In a large skillet, fry bacon and onions until almost done. While this is cooking, combine flour and spices on a plate. Rinse off shad roe and sprinkle with lemon juice. Dredge roe in flour mixture and place in skillet with bacon. Turn heat up to medium high, cover, and cook for 5 minutes. (Roe is done when inside is no longer red). Sprinkle with parsley and serve with lemon, bacon and onions.

Yield: 2 servings. Calories: 338 per serving.

SAUTEED ROCKFISH

¼ cup margarine
3 cloves garlic, crushed
¾ teaspoon lemon pepper
½ teaspoon oregano
½ teaspoon salt
2 pounds rock or trout fillets
½ cup vermouth
½ cup fresh parsley, chopped

Preheat electric skillet or frying pan to medium heat. Melt margarine, add garlic and spices and saute for 5 minutes. Add fish, increase heat to medium high and cook until halfway done. Add vermouth and turn fish. Continue cooking until done. Stir in parsley and serve.

Yield: 6 servings. Calories: 251 per serving.

ORIENTAL FISH SOUP

6 cups water
1 chicken breast
1 cup leeks, white part only, sliced
2 teaspoons fresh ginger, grated
1 cup leeks, sliced
1 cup bean sprouts
1 cup carrots, shredded
1 cup raw spinach, chopped
4 ounces bamboo shoots, fresh or
   canned
4 ounces water chestnuts, sliced
pinch white pepper
6 drops hot sauce
2 tablespoons soy sauce
3 tablespoons sherry
1 pound fish fillets, cut in chunks (trout
   or rock)

Simmer chicken, 1 cup white leeks and ginger in water for about two hours. Remove cooked leeks and ¼ cup of stock and puree in blender. Add this back to the stock and remove chicken. Add remaining vegetables, pepper, sauces and sherry. Simmer for 10 minutes. Add fish and simmer just until cooked. Serve with soy sauce and chow mein noodles.

Yield: 4 servings. Calories: 215 per serving.

Crepe Batter:
⅔ cup flour
2 small eggs, beaten
½ cup skim milk
1 tablespoon oil
pinch salt and pepper
1½ teaspoons oil for frying

Filling:
12 ounces trout fillets
½ cup fresh parsley, chopped
1 cup fresh mushrooms, sliced
¼ cup black olives, sliced
½ tablespoon margarine
2 tablespoons white wine
3 tablespoons low calorie mayonnaise
⅛ teaspoon each pepper, persillade
½ teaspoon salt
¼ teaspoon beau monde

Sauce:
1 can cream of mushroom soup
½ can water
¼ cup fresh mushrooms
pinch white pepper
paprika for sprinkling

Preheat oven to 350°F. Combine batter ingredients in a small bowl, mix well and set aside. In a shallow casserole dish, combine fillets, parsley, mushrooms, olives, margarine and wine. Cover and bake for 10-15 minutes. In a bowl, combine mayonnaise with spices. Drain fish and vegetables and add them to the mayonnaise mixture, stirring gently. Place in a warm oven until ready to use. Brush a 6″ diameter skillet lightly with oil. Pour 1½ tablespoons of batter in skillet, swirl around until it covers the skillet and fry until golden, turning once. Place crepes between paper towels in a warm oven. Prepare sauce by combining ingredients in a sauce pan and heat until boiling. Spoon about 2 tablespoons of filling on crepe shell, roll up and pour sauce over each. Sprinkle with paprika.

Yield: 5 servings, 2 crepes each. Calories: 324 per serving.

SQUID SKEWERS

1 pound squid, cleaned and cut into
¾" x 1½" strips
3 large green peppers, cut in small
chunks
1 20-ounce can pineapple chunks
1 cup grated parmesan cheese
50 4" wooden skewers

Microwave *(See page 35 "Terms for Microwaving")*:
Put squid piece on a skewer by placing one end of squid on the skewer and gathering it back and forth on the skewer. Each skewer should be prepared in the following order: squid, pepper, squid, pineapple, squid. Roll skewer in cheese and place 15 at a time on a plate. Microwave 1-2 minutes on roast or until squid turns a milky white. Remove those skewers that are done and continue cooking in 20 second increments until all are done.

Yield: 50 skewers. Calories: 17 calories each.

CRAB CALAMARI COCKTAIL

⅓ pound Maryland backfin crabmeat,
cartilage removed
⅓ pound squid, cleaned and cut into
½" squares
2 teaspoons lemon juice
⅓ teaspoon salt
1 tablespoon fresh parsley, chopped
⅛ teaspoon pepper
Romaine or lettuce
Celery sticks

Cocktail sauce:
½ cup tomato puree
1½ teaspoons worcestershire sauce
½ teaspoon sugar
3 drops hot sauce
¾ teaspoon horseradish
⅛ teaspoon seafood seasoning

Conventional oven:
Cook squid by dropping a few pieces at a time into boiling water and removing as soon as squid turns a milky white (6-10 seconds). Place squid in a bowl with crabmeat, sprinkle with lemon juice, salt, parsley and pepper. Cover and refrigerate until chilled (at least 1 hour). Mix together all sauce ingredients in a small bowl and chill. When ready to serve, cover 5 individual salad plates with romaine or lettuce. Place cocktail sauce in cocktail cups and garnish with celery sticks. Place in center of plate. Arrange seafood around sauce. Garnish with lemon slices. Serve cold.

Microwave *(See page 35 "Terms for Microwaving")*:
Place squid pieces on a large plate. Microwave for 30 seconds on high. Remove pieces that are done (turns milky white). Microwave the remaining pieces for 30 more seconds on high. Repeat until all squid is cooked. Follow above procedures for chilling and serving.

Yield: 5 servings. Calories: 66 per serving including cocktail sauce.

¼ pound fresh broccoli flowerettes
¼ pound fresh cauliflower
1 large green pepper, cut in short strips
1 medium squash, cut in thin, short strips
1 medium sweet potato, cut in thin slices
1 pound squid, cleaned and cut in ¼″ rings
2 quarts peanut or salad oil

Tempura Batter:
2 eggs, separated
¾ cup beer
1 tablespoon olive oil
1 cup flour
⅓ teaspoon salt
¼ teaspoon lemon pepper
⅛ teaspoon onion powder

Sweet n Sour Sauce:
½ cup brown sugar, packed
1 tablespoon cornstarch
¼ cup white vinegar
2 tablespoons red wine
⅓ cup chicken broth
¼ teaspoon ginger
¼ teaspoon garlic powder
1 tablespoon soy sauce

Arrange cut vegetables and squid on one large or several small platters. Prepare tempura batter by combining egg yolks, beer, oil, flour and spices in a medium bowl. Mix well. In a small bowl, beat egg whites until stiff. Gently fold whites into batter. Heat oil in a deep fryer or fondue pot to 375°F. Alternate vegetables and squid on fondue forks and dip into batter, drain extra batter, then fry in oil. Remove squid as soon as it turns a milky white (less than 1 minute). Cook vegetables to desired texture. Drain on paper towels and serve with a prepared mustard sauce and/or sweet and sour sauce.

In a medium sauce pan, combine all sauce ingredients and simmer over medium heat until sauce thickens. Makes 1¼ cups sauce.

Yield: 6 servings. Calories: 182 per serving.

PORTUGESA CALAMARI

1 pound squid, cleaned and cut into ¾″ squares
1 medium onion, finely chopped
2 garlic cloves, minced
4 tablespoons olive oil
¼ teaspoon sugar
4 shakes crushed red pepper
salt, to taste
2 bay leaves
2 tablespoons fresh parsley, chopped
2 16-ounce cans whole tomatoes, cut up
½ cup red wine
6 medium boiled potatoes, quartered

In a 2 quart sauce pan, saute squid, onion and garlic in olive oil for 5 minutes. Add remaining ingredients except for wine and potatoes and simmer for 30 minutes on medium high heat. Add wine and simmer over low heat for 30-40 more minutes. Sauce should be medium thick. Serve over boiled potatoes.

Yield: 6 servings. Calories: 293 per serving including potatoes.

EEL ASPARAGUS AU GRATIN

2 pounds eel fillets (dark membrane removed, cut to the length of an asparagus spear)
2 10-ounce boxes (about 30 spears) frozen asparagus spears, thawed
2 cups plain lowfat yogurt
1 cup Longhorn part skim cheese, shredded
1 cup Monterey Jack cheese, shredded
¼ cup dried chives
1 teaspoon salt
2 teaspoons brown sugar
pinch cayenne pepper
¼ cup sherry
paprika for garnish

Preheat oven to 375°. Place eel fillets over asparagus lengthwise in a lightly oiled baking dish (asparagus side down). Mix together remaining ingredients in a small bowl. Pour over eel and bake for 7-10 minutes, just until spears are tender and eel is cooked.

Yield: 6 servings. Calories: 570 per serving.

EEL SCALLOPINI

1 tablespoon oil
½ pound mushrooms, quartered
¼ cup green onion, chopped
2 tablespoons fresh parsley, chopped
1 clove garlic, crushed
2 pounds eel fillets, membrane removed, 1½" long strips
¼ cup margarine
1 tablespoon plus 1 teaspoon flour
1 teaspoon lemon juice
1 cube chicken bouillon
⅔ cup boiling water
½ cup sherry
2 teaspoons catsup
⅛ teaspoon pepper

Saute mushrooms, onion, parsley and garlic in oil in a large skillet for 3-4 minutes. Add eel and cook over medium-low heat for 5 minutes, turning once. While eel is cooking, melt margarine in a small sauce pan over low heat. Add flour and blend well. Turn heat up to medium and add lemon juice. Dissolve bouillon cube in boiling water and add to flour mixture. Add sherry, catsup and pepper and stir until well blended. Pour sauce over eel and let simmer over medium-high until hot.

Yield: 6 servings. Calories: 483 per serving.

1½ tablespoons oil
12 medium fresh mushrooms, sliced
1 8½-ounce can artichoke hearts, halved
1 pound eel fillets (dark membrane removed)
3 tablespoons margarine
2 tablespoons flour
1 cup white wine
½ cup skim milk
¼ teaspoon tarragon
2 teaspoons dried parsley
2 teaspoons fine herbs
paprika for garnish

Conventional oven:
Preheat oven to 375°F. Saute mushrooms and artichoke hearts in oil for 4-5 minutes. Arrange eel fillets in a baking dish. Add mushrooms and artichokes. In a small sauce pan, melt margarine over medium heat. Blend in flour and stir until bubbly. Add wine, milk and spices and stir until slightly thickened. Pour sauce over eel and vegetables, sprinkle with paprika and bake in oven for 15-20 minutes until eel is tender.

Microwave (See page 35 "Terms for Microwaving"):
(Omit oil for microwave recipe). Place mushrooms and artichoke hearts in a shallow dish and microwave for 5 minutes on roast. Cover and set aside. In a shallow casserole dish, melt margarine on roast for 2 minutes. Blend in 2½ tablespoons flour. Add wine and milk, cover with plastic and microwave on roast for 8 minutes, stirring several times. Stir in spices. Add eel and vegetables and microwave on roast for 6-8 minutes until eel is tender.

Yield: 4 servings. Calories: 460 per serving (baked). 415 per serving (microwave).

¾ pound or 12 whole squid, cleaned
2 tablespoons margarine
2 tablespoons flour
⅔ cup plain, lowfat yogurt
1 tablespoon fresh parsley, finely chopped
1 teaspoon sage
½ cup Port Wine cheese, grated
2 egg yolks, beaten
Italian bread crumbs for sprinkling
chopped pimento for garnish

Conventional oven:
Preheat broiler. Arrange squid on a lightly oiled baking dish. In a medium sauce pan, melt margarine and blend in flour. Stir in yogurt, parsley, sage and cheese. Set on medium heat, stir until cheese has melted. Remove from heat and add egg yolks a little at a time. Spread cheese mixture evenly over each squid. Sprinkle with Italian bread crumbs and garnish with pimento. Broil for 3-4 minutes.

Microwave (See page 35 "Terms for Microwaving"):
In a glass bowl, microwave margarine on roast for 50 seconds. Blend in flour. Add yogurt, parsley, sage and cheese. Cover and microwave for 3-5 minutes on roast until mixture is creamy. Stir in egg yolk and microwave 1 minute on roast. Spread mixture on squid pieces, in a square casserole dish, garnish and microwave for 4-6 minutes on roast, rotating pieces 3-4 times.

Yield: 4 servings. Calories: 227 per serving.

Fish should be frozen the same day it is caught or purchased due to its high perishability. Thawed seafood should not be refrozen.

The quality of the frozen product depends on how it was handled prior to freezing. Freezing only preserves quality, it does not improve it. If you are ever in doubt about the quality of the seafood, do not freeze it.

The best way to store fresh fish is to wrap it tightly in plastic wrap or freezer wrap, place it in an air-tight bag and seal. Place the bag in the vegetable keeper of your refrigerator and cover the bag with ice. Plan to use the fish within four days. If fresh fish is not surrounded by ice, it should be used within two days.

Most seafood may be stored in the freezer for three to six months depending on the species. It is important to remember that continued storage tends to dry out the product and causes deterioration in the quality and flavor. Labeling the package with the date and species prior to freezing will enable you to use the products in the proper order. Remove inedible parts, such as entrails, head and scales.

FREEZING FISH

Clean and dress fish and wash thoroughly. Wrap tightly in double thickness of plastic wrap, freezer bags or containers designed for freezing. Small fish can be frozen in a can or carton filled with water although this requires longer thawing times and it is not the best way to preserve flavor. Wrap fish in serving size portions for easier separation and thawing.

Freezing of the whole, uncleaned fish is not recommended.

FREEZING SHELLFISH

Shellfish are very delicate and perishable. Once they are removed from the water, they should be kept alive and under refrigeration until cooked or prepared for freezing. When freezing shucked seafood in containers, be sure to cover the seafood with water or seafood liquor to prevent freezer burn. Be sure to leave a 1/2 inch head space at the top for expansion. When freezing: Package only the amount of food that can be used at one time.

FREEZING CRABS

If you have leftover crabs or want to freeze crabmeat, follow these directions: Steam crabs, if not already cooked, for 25-30 minutes over boiling, salted water. Once cooled, remove back shell and break crab in half (front to back) and shake out the viscera. Thoroughly clean crab under running water. Remove any newly formed shell (a jelly-like substance with dark pigment). Pick the meat out of the body and claws.

The crabmeat is now ready for freezing. Although many consumers freeze fresh crabmeat just as it comes out of the can or shell, we suggest freezing it in a prepared dish such as crab cakes, crab imperial or crab soup. Crabmeat tends to become "tough," watery, and loses some of its flavor when frozen. Freezing hard shell whole crabs is not recommended. Sections of the crab body containing meat may be frozen and later used for soups.

Soft shell crabs can be frozen successfully. They should be dressed when still alive. Cut off the face behind the eyes, remove the apron, gills, stomach and intestines. Rinse in cold water and drain off. Wrap individually in tight fitting plastic film.

FREEZING CLAMS

Allow clams to stand in cool water or a weak salt solution for about half an hour to remove grit. Shuck clams and wash the meat thoroughly in cool water. Hard clams may be frozen in the shell. The shells should be tightly closed to indicate they are alive.

To freeze shucked clams, remove any bits of shell that may be present. Pour clam liquor over clams to cover completely in a rigid container. Leave a 1/2 inch head space and seal, label and date. Package only the amount that can be used at one time.

To freeze shucked breaded soft clams, coat the cleaned, shucked clam with a dry mix such as pancake mix. Blanch by cooking coated clams in hot oil (350°F.) for one minute. Drain on paper towels. Arrange blanched clams on a shallow tray and place in freezer until clams are stiff. Put frozen clams in a freezer bag, exhaust air, seal and freeze.

FREEZING OYSTERS

Fresh oysters should be washed and removed from the shell. Drain, wash in mild salt water solution and drain again. Pack oysters in liquid or water to completely cover them. Leave 1/2 inch head space and seal. Oysters may also be frozen in the shell. Place the oysters in a freezer bag, exhaust air and seal. These oysters are best used in soups and stews.

Freezing oysters in a prepared dish such as Oysters Florentine or Oysters Marinara may result in a better quality than the raw frozen oysters in natural juices.

Oysters may turn a different color during freezing as a result of the rapid change in temperature. They are still safe for consumption.

FREEZING SHRIMP

Previously frozen and thawed shrimp should not be refrozen. This causes a loss in flavor and texture change. Previously frozen shrimp that has thawed may be refrozen after cooking.

FREEZING SCALLOPS

Fresh scallops should be frozen in an air-tight, moisture-proof container. Pack scallops closely together and exhaust as much air as possible.

FREEZING LOBSTER

If you are going to freeze lobster, freeze only the parts containing meat if in the raw form. Remove the tail and claws and wrap tightly in moisture proof freezer wrap and freeze. Cooked lobster meat may be frozen. Follow the same procedures.

DEFROSTING

Fish does not have to be defrosted prior to cooking. For a quick main dish, just cook separated frozen fillets and increase the cooking time (see Cooking Times in the Bluefish section).

Thawing is recommended if fish will be stuffed, breaded or cooked with a sauce. Proper defrosting holds in the delicate flavor preserved by freezing the fish. Breaded and battered seafoods should not be defrosted before cooking.

Fish can be thawed by either of the following methods:

1. Defrost in the refrigerator. Allow frozen seafood to thaw overnight with a liner underneath. Large whole fish will take longer to thaw.

2. Thaw under cold running water. Allow 1/2 hour for each pound of frozen product.

Remember to keep seafood in its original wrapper until thawed. Do not defrost at room temperature or in warm water. This may spoil the fish if thinner edges thaw out more quickly than the thicker parts. Cook the fish within 2 days after it is defrosted. Do not refreeze.

Nutrition for the dollar should be a most important consideration when choosing foods for your family. It is even better if you can choose nutritious foods that are economical, easily attainable and tasty. This description fits seafood when in season and at peak quality.

Seafood is excellent in terms of nutrition because it has a high nutrient density. Nutrient density is the amount and variety of nutrients in 100 calories of food. For example, sugar would be considered to have a low nutrient density because although it provides carbohydrates, it does not provide any other nutrients. Seafood, on the other hand, is packed with high quality protein, many essential vitamins and minerals, water and some essential polyunsaturated fatty acids. When 100 calories of finfish is compared to 100 calories of ground beef, the finfish provides a higher amount of protein, calcium, phosphorus, potassium, sodium, vitamin A, thiamin and riboflavin, and a smaller amount of fat. (This is based on an average of 26 species of finfish, both lean and fatty). Seafood is also more easily digested than other meats, which is an important consideration for the very young and the elderly.

Seafood is an excellent source of high quality protein. It also contains trace minerals such as zinc, copper, iodine, manganese, cobalt, molybdenum and selenium, all of which are needed by

the body in small amounts. Of the water soluble vitamins, seafood is a good source of vitamin B6, B12, biotin, thiamin, riboflavin and folic acid. Fish oils are very high in fat soluble vitamins A and D. (The vitamin and mineral content varies with species, age, season, and geographical area).

The protein content of fish varies from 15-24% depending on the species and the time of year. Shellfish usually have less muscle protein than finfish, but the protein in all seafood is of very high quality. This means that the protein is complete with all the essential amino acids needed by our bodies. Shellfish protein varies with the season especially during spawning times. Protein and fat content are highest just before spawning and decrease after spawning.

The association between different types of fat in the diet and heart disease is still controversial. But, most health researchers today advocate a lessening of the amounts of saturated fats in our diet. Seafood, in general, contains very much less fat than most red meats and, more importantly, the fat contained in seafood is polyunsaturated.

Fish can be divided into two categories: lean and fatty.

Lean fish have less than 5% fat and more than 15% protein. Some seafood in this group include crabs, bluefish, carp, rockfish, halibut, croaker, sea bass, tuna, cod, haddock, flounder, pollock, mullet, ocean perch, whiting, scallops, squid, lobster, sea herring, snapper and sole.

Fatty fish contain more than 5% fat. Some species in this group include salmon, anchovies, mackerel, eel, and whitefish. Even though these fish contain more fat than the lean ones, they still contain 20% less fat than most red meats.

CALORIES

In general, seafood products are much lower in calories than other animal products. Many people are concerned with their weight and calorie intakes. Seafood makes an excellent high quality protein dish, that is tasty as well as low in calories.

CALORIE COMPARISON CHART

Item	Calories per ounce
Bluefish	33
Blue Crab	27
Perch	34
Scallops	23
Lobster	26
Beef Roast (rump)	73
Ham	87
Pork Chops	85
Chicken (white meat)	52

SEAFOOD STORAGE CHART

	REFRIGERATOR		FREEZER	
	COOKED	UNCOOKED	COOKED	UNCOOKED
Clams, in shell (hard & soft)	2-3 days	2-4 days[1]	—	3 mos.[2]
Clams, shucked (hard & soft)	1-2 days	1-2 days	3-6 mos.[3]	—
Crabs, steamed in shell	5-7 days	—	3 mos.[4]	—
Crabs (soft shell)	3-5 days	2-3 days (dressed)	3 mos.	3-6 mos.
Crabmeat, pasteurized, opened	3-5 days	—	3 mos.[5]	3-6 mos.[5]
Crabmeat, pasteurized, unopened	6 mos.	—	—	—
Crabmeat, fresh	3-5 days	3-5 days	3 mos.[5]	6 mos.[4]
Finfish, fatty (dressed or fillet)	2-3 days	1-2 days	3 mos.	3 mos.
Finfish, lean (dressed or fillet)	2-3 days	1-2 days	3 mos.	3-6 mos.
Fish roe	2-3 days	3-4 days	—	3 mos.
Lobster Tail	3-5 days	2-3 days[6]	3 mos.	3-6 mos.
Oysters, in shell	—	5-7 days	—	3 mos.
Oysters, shucked	5-7 days	7-10 days	—	6 mos.
Shrimp, headed & deveined	3-5 days	1-2 days	3 mos.	3-6 mos.
Squid, cleaned	3-5 days	2-3 days	3 mos.	3-6 mos.

Dashes (—) indicate "Not Recommended" or "does not apply."

(1) Shucked soft shell clams turn red as a result of ingesting certain seasonal algae. Some clams may change color overnight, others after 2 or 3 days. To avoid color change, use clams as soon as possible.

(2) Soft shell clams in shell do not freeze well, hard shell may be frozen. Use for soups or stews.

(3) Shucked clams should be in a semi-prepared form, e.g., par-fried.

(4) Meat containing section of the whole crab may be frozen. Freezing the whole crab is not recommended. Only cook live crabs.

(5) Crabmeat should be in a prepared dish (crab cake, crab casserole, etc.).

(6) If you have live lobster, cook while alive. If it dies during storage, remove tail and claws and cook immediately. (Discard body).

Note: These are average storage times based on proper handling of seafood prior to and during storage.
See section on freezing seafood for proper handling techniques.

EDIBILITY PROFILE CHART

This Edibility Profile categorizes seafood in two groups: Finfish and Shellfish. Each list is a group of seafood similar in edibility. If you like one fish from a list, you will probably like the others in that same list because of comparable color and flavor.

FINFISH

White meat, very light, delicate flavor	White meat, light to moderate flavor	Light meat, very light, delicate flavor	Light meat, light to moderate flavor	Light meat, light to moderate flavor	Light meat, more pronounced flavor	Darker meat, light to moderate flavor
Cabrilla, Spotted	Butterfish	Bass, Giant Sea	Bass, Striped	Pompano	Mackerel, Atlantic	Bluefish
Cod	Catfish	Bluegill	Buffalofish	Rockfish	Mackerel, King	Pout, Ocean
Cusk	Cobia	Crappie, White	Burbot	Sablefish	Mackerel, Spanish	Salmon, Chinook
Flounder, Southern	Flounder, Arrowtooth	Grouper	Carp	Salmon, Atlantic	Mullet, Redeye	Salmon, Red
Flounder, Summer	Flounder, Winter	Perch, Pacific Ocean	Chub, Lake	Salmon, Chum	Runner, Blue	Seabass, Black
Flounder, Witch	Lingcod	Pollock, Alaska	Croaker	Salmon, Coho		Sockeye
Flounder, Yellowtail	Mahi Mahi	Seabass, White	Drum, Black	Salmon, Pink		
Haddock	Plaice, American	Smelt	Eel	Sculpin		
Halibut, Pacific	Sauger	Sturgeon, Shovelnose	Jack, Crevalle	Scup		
Sanddab, Pacific	Seatrout, Spotted	Tautog	Jewfish	Shark, Sand		
Snapper, Yellowtail	Seatrout, White	Trout, Brook	Herring, Lake	Sheepshead		
Sole, Dover	Snapper, Red	Trout, Rainbow	Monkfish	Snapper, Vermillion		
Sole, Petrale	Snook	Walleye	Mullet	Spot		
Sole, Rex	Sole, English		Perch	Sturgeon, Lake		
Whitefish, Lake	Triggerfish, Gray		Perch, Atlantic	Turbot, Greenland		
	Whiting		Pike, Northern	Trout, Lake		
	Whiting, Pacific		Pollock			
	Wolffish					

SHELLFISH

Crabs	Shrimp	Crawfish	Lobsters	Univalves	Bivalves	Bivalves	Cephalopods
Alaska King	Blue	Freshwater Crayfish	American	Abalone	Clams:	Oysters:	Octopus
Blue	Brown	Sea Crawfish	Rock	Conch	Butter	Eastern/ Atlantic	Squid
Dungeness	California Bay	Western Crayfish	Slippery	Snails:	Geoduck	Gulf	
Jonah	Northern		Spiny	Sea Snails	Hard (Quahog)	Olympic	
Red	Rock			Cockles	Littleneck	Pacific	
Snow	White				Pismo	S. Amer.	
Soft Shell					Razor		
Tanner					Soft	Scallops:	
					Surf (Skimmer)	Bay	
					Mussels:	Calico	
					Blue	Sea	
					California		